Bank on Your
Smart Device
2026

Bank on Your Smart Device 2026

Jerome Svigals

To order additional copies of this book, contact:
Xlibris
1-888-795-4274
www.Xlibris.com
Orders@Xlibris.com
735937

CONTENTS

IV. Smart Devices and New Markets

Preface

The banking world is quickly evolving from an era of Electronic Banking, based on plastic cards and readable checks, to a new era of Digital banking. It will center on hand-held, mobile communication based and stored program operated transaction Devices (Smart Devices). It will communicate via networks, primarily the world wide Internet.

This report is intended to help you understand the use of Smart Devices on the Internet in preparing for Retail Banking 2026. This preface is intended to introduce you to the Internet and its role, in the Digital banking era.

Action

Each Chapter will offer you a succinct identification of the actions you will need to use the recommendations of that Chapter. Use the content of this preface to prepare to organize, orient and activate your resources to realize the benefits of using Smart Devices on the Internet, in order to achieve Digital banking actions and results

A Note of Interest

"Internet Changes Brains: . . . . Internet training stimulates neural activation patterns and enhances brain function and cognition". This quote is taken from a study by a Professor of psychiatry at the Institute for Neuroscience and Human Behavior at UCLA.

Projection

Projecting the use of Smart Devices for a decade forward requires dealing with the Digital banking era's new technologies and new business concepts. This projection will focus on two important improvements. They are: (1) the role of the Internet; and (2) the implementation of a Smart Device based electronic banking set of processes and media. Start with a brief glossary of new terms.

The Internet

A technical definition: The "Internet" is a worldwide network of computer based communication systems which use a common protocol to facilitate data transmission. A "Protocol" is a set of rules for determining the format and for controlling the transmission of data. A "network" is an interconnected system of electronically connected digital Devices.

A societal definition: The "Internet" is a world wide information super highway providing access to many data bases. A "data base" is an organized collection of information. The organization identifies the content and method of access to the content. Smart Devices give access to banking data bases which combine specifics of customers accounts and the processing of bank managed media such as funds transfer transactions (formerly checks) and contracted services such as loans.

A practical definition: The "Internet" is an access Device to the world's information. The challenge is to know how to reach the desired content. Tools such as "Search" programs and scanning or "Browser" programs provide organized access to this broad array of information. Exercising these tools with Smart Devices produces a stream of information which must be examined and evaluated for usefulness. Using the specific address (URL) of an Internet information source (Web Page) by-passes the need to exercise a search program and takes you directly to the designated Web page. It also by-passes and eliminates the need to examine the stream of search results.

The URL:

(Uniform Resource Locator—The Global address of documents and other resources on the world wide web (the Internet).

The URL, entered through a Smart Device to a Browser, takes the user directly to a desired Internet Web Page. In the case of a banker it can take you directly to the bank customer's records and available resources. In a health application the URL can take you directly to the patient's health record and doctor's orders. In a retail application it can take you directly to a sales offer and the Web page for recording order specifics. In any industry application the URL entered through the Smart Device can take you directly to the user's personal data and status accessed through the Internet.

Internet Marketing

A key element of future Smart Device activities will be use of the Internet to achieve business objectives. For example, "Internet Marketing" will be the offering of goods and services through the information distribution functions available with the "Information Super Highway". There are entire industries being developed to achieve these marketing goals. These include promoting products or services, and providing for customers' Smart Device access to options such as bank accounts and required transactions. In retail it captures order size, quantity, style in capturing the specific order from the customer with payment and shipping instructions.

Digital banking

A major example of Smart Device implementation in Internet based business is "Digital banking". Smart Device based Digital banking is intended to handle "value information", e.g. monetary value, for savings and transaction accounts. It also uses value information via Smart Devices for making loans, transferring value and creating credit instruments.

Digital banking is performing the business of banking through the use of Smart Device accessed Internet facilities. This requires creating an information alternative for each of the physical instruments used in the conventional bank. These may include checks, credit and transaction cards, passbooks, mortgages, bonds, contracts and so forth. These new

Smart Device based electronic value information instruments will be described in this all electronic Digital banking environment.

The Forces for Smart Device Based Industry Change

Society continually undergoes changes resulting from actual experiences. The real question is how many of the players realize changes are taking place. Changes sometimes seem to occur slowly and, except for the most observant observers, are nor perceived or understood. The forces for change discussed here are representative of the new changes that will greatly improve performance of the Internet and Smart Device based electronic communication functions during the next decade.

The Impact of Change:

Note that the perception of change requires an understanding of the impact of change on business processes. That is, it takes a good knowledge of business processes to perceive the impact of change. The following functional events are considered to be the most significant changes impacting the next decade. In my opinion time will confirm these changes.

Lessons From Magnetic Striped Card Based Self-Service

Historically, the bank industry has been an aggressive user of new solutions and technologies as they were developed. A good example is the adoption of the international standard magnetic striped transaction card which were first used by American Express and American Airlines in 1970 with the advent of the large scale Boeing 747 airplane. Their function was to cope with the large increase in the number of passengers. These magnetic striped cards were intended to serve as transaction cards in a variety of self-service units. These included self-service reservations, ticketing and in access Devices including employee identification and access control.

Magnetic Stripe Usage Today

Today, less than 50 years later, use of the striped media has spread to 80% of the world's population and in all industries. Striped media are used in mass transit ticketing, driver's licenses, access control, and on later generation Smart (EMV) cards for transition and backup purposes. They were first used with self-service cash dispensers and later with Automatic Teller Machines. The latter adding a second currency dispenser and a depository to a cash dispenser.

There are also families of "Point-of-sale" units used in a wide variety of retail establishments. They combine slot type stripe readers with bar code readers for item tags and identification. These entries are supplements with manual entries by the clerk for transaction options such as quantities. The operation of these units has been organized so that they are understood and implementable by relatively unskilled clerks.

Why The Broad Usage of Striped Cards?

The important question is why was there such broad acceptance and use of magnetic striped cards? The secret is NOT in the stripe. The secret is a combination of two factors. First, the striped cards have been designed for ease of holding and handling. The stripe and its orientation are easily recognized on the card surface. It provides for a simply understood direction of insertion into the accepting unit. When the operation is completed the card is returned to a position where it easily can be grasped and removed.

In some units, such as Automatic Teller Machines, the card must be removed before the currency is dispensed. That overcomes the problem of currency removal and then forgetting to take away the card. That was a common problem in early dispenser units. A better solution is to never let go of the card. A slot reader offers ease of orientation. In operation the user never releases the card from the hand. Hence, there is very high probability that the user will not leave the card in the accepting unit.

The second reason for striped card wide acceptance and use is in the operation of the accepting unit. The accepting machine process has been simplified to where it is understood by the user in one use or one demonstration of the unit. In technical terms that is called a "Learning Curve of One". This is the challenge to the future Internet based, Smart Device based, Digital banking processes. They must be structured to achieve a "Learning Curve of One" as experienced by the user of the process. Achieving that goal means that there is a high probability that the user will be successful in achieving a complete transaction in a subsequent self-service and unattended mode of operation without additional help.

Why Self Service ?

The self-service mode of processing business transactions offers significant improvements over attended transactions. These transactions reduce labor costs. They allow 24/7 hours of operations. They permit access from remote and unattended locations other than conventional branch premises. Studies indicate that self-service offers faster transactions with up to 40% improvement.

Self-service banking is an obvious use of Smart Devices and other mobile transaction Devices. These transactions are easily used for monitoring account balances, paying bills, and transferring funds. There are a growing number of portable Devices with camera functions that capture check images for remote deposits. Also available are a diverse important security functions that function with self-service transactions.

Successful Internet and Smart Device based transactions will need to satisfy the following prime lesson for self service from prior card usage success. The Internet transactions will need to be structured so that they are easily understood and implemented with a "Learning Curve of One". Past performance shows that the industry understands this need. Further, it has demonstrated that they have the ability to satisfy this important usage criteria.

Deployment of Compact Communications Units

A recent study found that 71% of children under 15 years of age are using mobile Devices for games and telephoning home. This is a formative experience for tomorrow's Internet and Smart Device based Digital banking customers. Simultaneously the communications units are acquiring complete electronic business "applications". These prepackage software solutions enable the Smart Device users to rapidly achieve electronic, self-service application functions and solutions.

The hand-held, mobile communications unit, or mobile Device, is now used by 5.0 billion people according to the International Telecommunications Union (ITU). More than 40% of the world's people have access to the Internet. Five hundred million of the Internet users have high speed access. In the United States Jupiter Research reports that over 1.5 billion people will use their mobile Devices to access banking and payment services by 2016. They are expected to implement millions of communications based banking transactions in the same period.

The Mobile Devices and Smart Devices

There are at least 10 major mobile Device types (CP). They share a number of functions. These include: Weather, Screen light, Electronic phonebook, Daily calendar, Data storage, To do lists, Multiple network attachment, Handheld Near Field Communications (NFC) contact, (Smart Device (CP) to CP), Companion unit synchronism, Games, and Google/Yahoo maps. Most have a "Blue Tooth" local, personal area network capability. They operate on a 2.45 GHZ frequency with a Spread Spectrum protocol and are low power and operating up to 32 feet with up to 8 other Devices simultaneously.

NFC technology is a standards-based wireless communications technology that permits data to be exchanged between Devices located a few inches apart. The technology is used in a large number of mobile Devices for a full range of mobile applications. These include making payments by waving a mobile Device close to another mobile Device or close to a point-of-sale set up to receive NFC signals. NFC enabled Devices are governed by ISO/IEC 18092 specifications published by the NFC Forum.

The mobile communications unit (usually a Smart Device) usually contains a portable computer with Internet interface. An added feature is optical capture. In many cases this feature is used to capture computer output display content for future portable usage. The Internet output provides data base access. This generated inquiry results in the form of tables and lists which are candidates for optical capture. In banking, the optical capture may be used to capture check images for check deposit processing without physically delivering the paper check to the depositor's bank.

The Mobile Device Applications

The mobile Devices include a keyboard or touch screen for data entry. Possible applications include electronic games, tutoring for Digital banking transactions, voice services, location based services, Internet access, messaging and social networking, live chatting, entertainment, commerce including banking; medicine including health monitoring, education and government broadcasting and reporting applications. Almost universally, the attachment of the hand-held communications Device is via an electronic signal or "wireless" attachment.

The New Smart Device Replaces the Card

Probably, the most important role for the hand-held communications unit will be the replacement of today's financial transaction plastic card. The earlier bank card serves three purposes. First, it identified the issuing institution and accepting network with displayed logos and text. The second function was to show specific control information such as expiration date, card type, e.g. credit or debit card, batch control information, and unique account number. The third function of the card was to contain machine readable information in the form of a recorded magnetic stripe content. All of these functions will be provided in the future by the hand-held, mobile, communications Device. It will be both visually readable by display and machine readable by electronic signals (e.g. Near Field Communications (NFC)).

Access to World Wide Communications

The world-wide Internet communications network provides for the interchange of packets of information. The packets move between individual "platforms". A platform is a combination of hardware and an operating system (software) and it provides the user with a method of accessing the Internet. These are, sometimes, an Internet Browser, which is a software package designed to seek a specific URL-based (Universal Resource Locator or Internet address) Web page. The "Web Page" is a textual collection of information which may be audio, visual, and/or graphical. The Web page may represent an individual bank customer's record or profile. It also may represent offerings or account status from a banking institution

Internet usage demonstrates the rate of its usage growth. Based on reports from the International Telecommunications Union (www. internetworldstats.com), current Internet usage and its growth are:

Geographic Area	% of Population Internet Users	10 Year Growth Internet Usage (past)
No America	74 %	132 %
Oceana/Australia	60	173
Europe	50	283
Latin America	30	873
Asia	19	516
Middle East	24	1360
Africa	7	1360
All	25 (1.7 Bln)	4,697

An interesting aspect of these Internet penetration statistics are the countries with the largest penetration of Internet users. They are:

Country	% of Population Internet Users	10 Year Growth Internet Usage (past)
United Kingdom	80 %	217 %
South Korea	77	97
Japan	74	100

| USA | 74 | 139 |

An interesting aspect of the USA Internet using population is that 18 to 44 year-olds comprise one half of the Internet-using population. Furthermore, youths dominate this group. 93% of 12 to 17 year-olds are online. This compares to 89% of 18 to 24 year-olds and 83% of those 40 to 44 years of age.

These Internet usage statistics suggest the reason why portable communication Devices are increasingly assuming application function. The new Smart Device customers are already conditioned to the new functional Devices in the marketplace. This is particularly important when considering the impact of the "Social" networks such as Twitter, Facebook, and up to 100 social networks, world-wide, which are gaining rapid acceptance with the Internet users.

Summary

Past self service functional evolution (Electronic Banking) has clearly established these future Internet application trends for Digital banking:

* Learning Curve of One usage development patterns will greatly encourage self-service usage by Internet customers.

* Hand-held communications units will be universally available and used for a wide variety of Internet applications.

* Communication facilities will be widely available and will enable electronic Internet activities to and from almost anywhere in the world.

These attributes describe the foundation on which "Smart Device Bank 2026" will be built.

Executive Summary

Purpose of this report: The banking world is quickly evolving from an era of Electronic Banking, based on plastic cards and readable checks, to a new era of Digital banking, based on hand-held, communication's based, stored program operated, transaction Devices (Smart Devices) communicating via networks, primarily the world wide Internet.

This report is intended to help you understand the use of Smart Devices on the Internet in preparing for BANK ON YOUR SMART DEVICE. It is intended to introduce you to the Internet and its role, in the Digital banking era.

Smart Device Concepts

The hand held communicating phone has introduced a new way of life. It offers walking and traveling conversation. Stand on any street corner, in any city at any time of the day and you will observe all classes of society going bye with a hand held communications Device being held next to their ear. Usage statistics claim more than 80% of the world's population have access to and use a communicating phone like Device. Their use ranges from socializing and safety to commercial and financial activities. The users range from 8 or 10 years old to immobile senior citizens seeking social interaction and a substitute for physical motion.

Smart Device Based Banking

The Smart Device is a hand-held, internet based, stored program computer which includes smart Device functions. The Internet is a world wide network of computer based communication systems, using a common information protocol. Market migration to an all electronic,

Smart Device based, digital banking concept will have significant impact on conventional banking facilities. It will impact the physical attributes of the bank branch. Tellers for face-to-face transaction processing will disappear as they are replaced by remote, communications based, self service, transactions. It will significantly change the roll of branch banking personnel. It will reduce physical efforts such as mail delivery and processing. It will replace physical money and check needs with network/electronic based secure functions and strategies. Visits to the "branch" for transactions will be accomplished electronically. The business of Smart Device based digital banking will be 24/7. Successful bankers will need to move rapidly to keep up with the rapidly changing, remote, electronic functional environmental marketplace.

Forces for Change

The forces for migration of the bank to a Smart Device based role change will include: (1) the rapid growth of mobile Devices and Smart Devices as the prime vehicles of individual communications, and their replacing transaction cards and checks; (2) the role of the Internet as the dominant world wide communications network in almost all industries including bank, health, retail, education and government; (3) the disappearance of paper in the bank industry, including the growth of electronic money, check images, and remote/interactive self service; and (4) the migration of bank based Smart Device systems from stand alone facilities to Cloud systems with the removal of all geographic and physical boundaries. A Cloud system is the user's portion of a larger, internet based, remote computer system.

Digital banking with Smart Devices

Digital bankingis the use of a portable communications Device to access and use financial services. This concept is well established with the use of wireless phones to find bank account balances and their status. As portable communications Devices evolved into Smart Devices, portable computers that allow phone calls, their banking functions are further increasing in sophistication. For example, Smart Devices are now being used to capture and transmit check images for electronic deposits. The portable Device also runs banking applications. For example, they can be used to calculate currency conversions and mortgage loan tables. Self service is the direct benefit of forty years of magnetic striped card based self service banking.

The Internet

The Internet allows access from more points, more quickly and more easily than any other network in the history of networks. Thus, along with its new facilities comes new and serious security exposures. Since there is no central authority dealing with these security exposures, the users must insure that they are protecting Internet plans and banking activity programs. Their actions must protect your Internet plans and programs. Seventy-five percent of Smart Device users are concerned about the loss exposure from lost and stolen Smart Devices. Please take this note of caution very seriously. There are security tools to protect your Internet actions. Your goal must be to use them effectively. (For detailed security material see Xlibris book "Secure Your Internet Use").

Card and Check Migration

Physical check entry to the bank disappeared with the advent of check image capture in ATM's, mobile Devices and Smart Devices. However, the real test is the process by which the individual originates a "check-like" based payment. The payment needs to identify the payer and the payee. Where bills are being paid, the payee is identified by the demand for payment. The optical image feature of the Smart Device can be used to capture that data just as it is used to capture check images for processing.

The Plastic Card Equivalent Transaction

Use of the digital banking Device as a magnetic striped card equivalent signal source requires a wireless transmission from the digital banking Device to the signal accepting unit. A NFC, (near field communications) signal is emitted by the digital banking Device. The digital banking Device displays multiple striped card equivalent type designations. A record is captured in the digital banking unit for later reference, if needed. The acceptance Device processes the "card-like" transaction into the banking system. The variable amount of the transaction is added to the signal transmitted in the NFC signal to the accepting Device. The complete transaction data is then processed by the banking system.

Smart Device and Cloud Computing

Smart Device based Cloud computing is the delivery of common Smart Device based bank business computer applications from a remote facility, online, through the Internet. These Smart Device based applications are accessed with a Web Browser. It uses software and data stored on servers (computer subsystems). The bank Cloud user rents a portion of the Cloud infrastructure from a third party. These Smart Device based Cloud processes reduce cost to the bank by sharing the Cloud computer power and resources. The bank does not have to provide added capacities for peak loads. The user must be concerned about the security of Cloud stored information and its protection.

Bank Organization of 2026

The primary, government-licensed, bank functional units (teller, loan and payments) will be the same in 2026. The primary changes of 2026 will be in the implementation of each function. The former implementation with paper based, manual processing and local handling will be replaced. They will be replaced by Smart Device based "electronic paper", electronic processing and remote Internet based processing. This will be achieved by the use of mobile transaction Devices, use of the world wide Internet, and electronic logic implementation Devices.

Internet Bank Accounts and Transactions

The all electronic bank of year 2026 will use the Internet to provide bank account records, access and all "branch" type functions and transactions for customers using the Internet. Smart Device based access to the 2026 bank, with all electronic accounts, will start with the URL (Internet address) of the Web page assigned to each customer's account. An explicit URL will be a unique Web page address for each customer's bank account. The customer's Web page, in turn, will provide direct access to all bank relations for that customer.

What is a Smart Device ?

The simple, hand held, portable telephone has evolved into a hand held computer, Internet based, and providing phone functions. It is the result of decades of electronic component functional growth and physical size reduction. The simple, hand-held, portable telephone has evolved to a compact, fist-sized, computer capable of 95% of the function of your desk top computer. Its portability reaches any place you can contact mobile Device electromagnetic signals. Its computational ability exercises any programmable computer application within the capability of its operational program system. In other words, the room full of computers in past decades now operate efficiently in your palm as a Smart Device. Furthermore, it has a full display, a keyboard, an operating system and communications interface.

Credit Card on a Phone

The Smart Device uses NFC (Near Field Communications) capability to communicate with a transaction acceptor. The Smart Device is brought within 4 inches (or 10 centimeters) of the acceptor. Select card equivalent information. Initiate the emission of a selected transaction card. This is equivalent to swiping a magnetic striped transaction card through a card slot reader. To enable this transaction, the Smart Device contained application is opened with keying in a pin or a biometric read, a personal identification number. The application allows loading the equivalent of multiple account information (card equivalents), within one Smart Device. This multiple account facility is used now in Southeast Asia countries and is spreading around the world. The NFC function allows two way communication. However, payment transactions are one way with account number going to the acceptor. Visa has tested this function in the United States and Southeast Asia.

Smart Device Applications

An application is a software program designed to produce a specific result or solution to an identified need. It may also be a computer configuration (input, computation and/or result use) designed to achieve a specific result. An application solution may also be the use of Smart Device functions and features designed to achieve a specific result.

Select and Execute an Application Program

Access the Smart Device's application directory for descriptions, prices, capacity requirements for storage and execution, display logo, network attachment, and performance needs. The selected applications are downloaded to the Smart Device. An identifying logo is displayed on the Smart Device display for later selection and execution. There are more than 450,000 Smart Device applications depending on the Smart Device and operating system you are using. To illustrate the range of applications, there is a list of the "must-own" Smart Device applications.

Familiarization (Based on the BlackBerry Smart Device).

Find the "On" button. It is generally in the lower right corner with a sun-like icon. It may also be a button in the upper left corner. When the button is depressed the screen becomes illuminated. The keyboard also becomes illuminated. Identify the speaker, microphone and earphone connection socket. On the reverse side find the removable cover for the battery and SIM card. The SIM card contains the information giving you access to a specific communications carrier and to a specific phone number. Moving the SIM card to another Smart Device gives it access to the identified phone number and carrier. Welcome to the world of thumb typing. Your thumbs enter information while the other fingers support the Smart Device.

Smart Device Politics (The authors opinion).

The fast and successful pace of Smart Device usage growth attracts a number of interested parties, especially those associated with previous technologies and market entries. All of the instruments associated with earlier solutions of the payment and marketing solutions will be impacted. Financial transaction cards, Smart (EMV) cards, ATMs, conventional retail marketing solutions, telephones, paper money, and face to face transactions. Aggressive, former industry groups will carve out a roll for them selves in this transition. For example, if their prior solution used integrated circuit chips, they will use that as evidence that they should automatically have a key role in the subsequent developments. That may not be entirely wrong. The Smart Device era will need standards.

The Unbanked and the Under Banked

Unbanked refers to any household or individual that does not make use of a financial institution for any type of financial or banking service or transaction. Under banked are small businesses with access to financial services but do not use them. The Unbanked are reported as 10% of USA population. Under banked are reported at an additional 15% of the USA population. These are currently reported as 28 million plus 45 million people. Both groups, the Unbanked and Under banked, spend $130 million per year on alternative but relatively expensive financial services. These include check cashing services, pay day loans and money transfer services. Both have been seen as future business opportunities by most bankers.

New Smart Device Banking Role and Revenues

A remarkable characteristic of the Internet is the amount of free material available to anyone. Some providers, like Google, have evolved a plan to get advertisers to pay for the free results provided to its users. That is very much like the payment by advertisers for free radio broadcast programs which clearly identify the sponsor. However, it is expected that some web providers in the future will expect payment for their content. Bank services are paid for by the bank's customers in the form of loan and mortgage payments and the use of deposits.

Micropayments

Future bank services may need transaction payment amounts which are smaller in value. Similarly, Internet providers will need to avail themselves of techniques for collecting a larger volume of smaller amounts in payments.

Smart Device Economics 2026

The bank of 2026 will be considerably different with staff use and facilities. That will not necessarily reduce the cost of providing the bank. There will be major changes in the mechanization and supporting personnel. The physical branches size will decrease significantly. However, there will be expenses associated with smaller service facilities and remote Cloud facilities. There will be more expenses associated with maintaining the software and data bases need to support the new branch equivalent virtualization structure. Moving to the all electronic bank will also move the bank to a 24 hour, seven days per week response organization. The bank structure will be much more unattended. However, that requires operating facilities, power on, with fully operable communications and network services. Money will go into facilities to support this type of operation, their operating and maintenance staffs.

Security Architecture

As an Internet user, you must understand your own requirements. As a user, you must provide key information such as credit card numbers. The merchant provides important information in the form of receipts and payment information. Vital data flows in both directions. Hence, your security objectives must describe your possible exposures and your planned responses. A security approach must be selected, implemented and the response evaluated for adequacy. Any solution will involve trade offs. The user must decide where to draw the line between expense and security adequacy. There will be new security solutions for the Smart Device/Internet environment.

PCI Security Standards Council

The Payment Card Industry Security Standards Council was founded by five global payment organizations. They are American Express, Discover Financial Services, JCB (Japan Card) International, MasterCard Worldwide, and Visa Inc. The PCI DSS has six major objectives. A formal information security policy must be defined, maintained, and followed at all times and by all participants

Who is Who in Smart Device Based Mobile Banking

This is a list of software suppliers at the time this report was prepared. It is important to repeat a search of the Internet for the most recent list when you are preparing to use this information. This is a fast moving industry. Only the most current of search results will provide you with a current list of software suppliers and available applications.

Keyless Internet Processes

Forty years experience with magnetic striped cards, used with self service units ranging from mass transit to Automatic Tellers, demonstrates why 80% of the world's population is implementing self-service transactions in all industries. By contrast, 72% of our population are shopping on the Internet, but only 15% shop with multiple vendors. The need is for a "Keyless Internet Transaction" structure which can be understood and repeated with ONE use. That was the prime success factor for magnetic striped card use. The "keyless" process is demonstrated.

Traveling with a Smart Device

Historically, traveling meant leaving your entertainment Devices at home—your music, your books, your reference materials, your movies and your TV. Today, they all travel with you, thanks to the Smart Device and networks. In addition, your Smart Device provides important assistance on your travels.

Smart Device User interface

The Smart Device display is the principle interface to the user. Its goal is to quickly communicate to the user the nature of the application and to enable quick user response for option selection, information entry and action initiation. As stated previously, the goal of effective user interaction is to achieve a "Learning Curve of One". The Smart Device display is probably the single most important element needed to achieve the "Learning Curve of One". This guide will try to provide suggestions to make more effective use of the display. They will highlight those display characteristics needed to aid in achieving that goal.

For Comments and Suggestions

Your questions, comments and suggestions about this report are invited.

Please send them to smartcard@sprynet.com.

I Smart Devices

Chapter i-1

Smart Device Concepts

Purpose: Introduce Smart Devices and their functions.

Action: Assist the reader in selecting a Smart Device.

Hand-Held, Communicating Phone Concepts:

The hand held, communicating mobile Device has introduced a new way of life. It offers walking and traveling conversation. Stand on any street corner, in any city at any time of the day and you will observe all classes of society going bye with a hand held communications Device being held next to their ear. Usage statistics claim more than 80% of the world's population have access to and use a communicating mobile Device like Device. Their use ranges from socializing and safety to commercial and financial activities. The users range from 8 years old to immobile senior citizens seeking social interaction and a substitute for physical motion. The communicating mobile Devices have unusual activities ranging from use by enemy fighters in Afghanistan to activate explosive Devices to use by students to seek quiz answers.

The Varieties of Communicating Mobile Devices

Definitions: The "Mobile Device" is a hand held Device providing audio communications through wireless attachment. The "Smart Device" is a hand held, programmable, Internet based computer which also provides mobile Device capabilities via wireless attachment. Other e-Device forms include iPads, iPhones, some forms of eBooks, computers on a wireless router and similar Devices. All of these alternatives share wireless attachment. The communications route may be conventional telephone networks or through the Internet. Smart Devices may use either communications network alternative. There will continue to be a stream of new Smart Device products, Smart Devices, and related e-Devices. The market will continue to demand new functions and improving economics. Smart Devices provide a variety of functions, including: a GPS/navigation Device; a radio; an e-reader; and a medical sensing Device. Usage will be as common as the pocket pen. There will be functional differences. Hence, the challenge to this report is to allow you to master the complete functional range of Smart Devices without giving you a unique driver's manual for each model.

Report Objectives:

The number and variety of communicating mobile Devices, and like Devices, are growing too fast to catalog all the Devices and options available. This treatise is intended to help you select and learn to drive this Device, independent of the specific brand and model you eventually choose. We will offer you the fundamentals. You will need to master them and then select a specific Smart Device version, closest to satisfying your communications and processing needs. This process will require that we cover a number of pertinent subjects ranging from types of Devices and to their range of functional options.

Effective use of Smart Devices will require understanding fundamentals such as what is a Smart Device, how does it know where you are, how may it be programmed to provide selected application alternatives, with what performance economics and how your information and its privacy may be protected in the usage. Smart Device use will change many industries transaction handling alternatives.

An important result of our previous "Retail Bank 2026" report observed changes will be the major reduction in branch face-to-face transaction traffic and space requirements. The bank branch will continue to be vital for customer acquisition and education in the 2026 Digital banking era transaction Devices and the new Internet processes. However, there will no longer be a need for face-to-face transaction tellers and related facilities such as Automatic Teller Machines and the physical space they formerly required. Hence, bank management will need to anticipate and prepare for the reduced space, changing personnel roles, equipment and supporting system's capacity that will no longer be required.

This report is intended to be a companion for the "Retail Bank 2026" report. Hence, its emphasis will be to provide the year 2026 retail banking functions. This will be a banking environment in which the use of the plastic transaction card (magnetic striped or Smart Card with an imbedded integrated circuit chip) will be replace by the emission and capture of equivalent information by a Smart Device. Likewise, the Smart Device operation will replace the presentation and use of paper checks or their equivalent documents, by the emission and capture of equivalent information. In both alternatives, use of the Internet for communications of the card/paper equivalent information provided will change the banking industry. The need for face-to-face financial transactions in a physical branch will be replaced by an electronic network based equivalent flow of information.

A Status Report for the Smart Device Banking Industry
(ref: Credit Suisse, Mobile Payments)

Mobile payments are projected to grow at 107% CAGR world wide. They originate with 4.6 billion mobile Devices. This population is growing at 1.6 billion mobile Devices per year.

Although the installed population is large, there are many deployment hurdles. First, is the number of alternative technologies available for remote communications. These include: MicroSD cards, Radio Frequency Identification (RFID) stickers, 2DBar codes, and Near Field Communications (NFC). There is a pressing need for a standardized solution with potential for up grading.

Payment networks are doing pilots with most major banks. They are aggressively pursuing mobile payments. The networks include Visa, MasterCard, Soft (formed by AT&T, T-Mobile (a Deutsche Telephone subsidiary), and Verizon), American Express and Discover. They are focusing on how to differentiate their services. All are trying to develop new mobile results and implementing know how with improved security. The networks are motivated by recent regulatory changes which have reduced their incomes, such as the reduced debit interchange fees. The Smart Device offers an improved way to produce new services incomes, by Smart Device applications, without a huge need for capital investment.

The payment networks collectively faces these challenges: Incorporating the NFC technology in all mobile Devices; providing the mobile servicers with part of the revenues being produced; getting more merchants to accept mobile services; getting more consumers to use mobile transactions and Devices; coping with the added competition from more mobile services; and providing adequate transaction security.

Consumers are accepting the new functionality faster than past Devices, according to the Tower Group study. Consider the number of years required to reach 100 million acceptors:

Actual:

Magnetic striped card:	28 years
Debit cards:	12 years
Paypal:	7 years
iPods:	6 years

Projected (from a Javelin study)

Contactless cards:	5 years
Mobile banking:	4 years
NFC Enabled Devices:	3 years

The key mobile Device functions today (according to a Javelin study):

Pay bills:	19 %
Transfer funds:	15 %

In-store purchases: 14 %

Real time purchases: 13 %

Online purchases: 11 %

Loan prepaid cards: 8 %

The mobile Device transactions use these applications: (From a Gartner Study):

	% Transactions	% $ Volume
Money transfer:	21 %	75 %
Prepaid card top up:	46	12
Ticketing:	11	1
Purchase merchandize:	11	9
Bill Pay:	6	2
Other:	5	1

The mobile technologies used (From a Gartner Study):

SMS Short Message Service:	67 %	79 %
NFC Near Field Commnctns:	30	5

The current popular banking choices (world wide, Javelin Study) percent of customers:

Android: 47 %

iPhone: 48 %

BlackBerry: 29 %

A new entry, the iPad is starting to be used for mobile payments (Credit Suisse estimates from company data):

	Worldwide	USA
2010 (Est)	8 %	6 %
2012 (Est):	25	6
2014 (Est):	46	22

International Experience:

Japan: Highly successful starting from a cash-intensive society. High mobile Device penetration with 70 % having payment capabilities.

Visa is currently running mobile pilots in over 18 countries and the United States. Some include real-time fraud monitoring and encryption technology to assure that mobile-initiated Visa transactions are as secure as other Visa payments. Visa also has 7 mobile payment international partnerships.

MasterCard has 20 international mobile partnerships. MasterCard uses a different technology than NFC. They us the Gemalto Upteq N-Flex mobile payment Device. This is comprised of a plastic strip wrapped around a SIM card.

China UnionPay (CUP) is conducting NFC pilots in 6 provinces. They expect to have hundreds of millions cardholders and 100,000 merchants capable of accepting mobile payments by the end of 2010. CUP is also working with a number of companies to up grade their point-of-sale units to the new NFC technology.

In the United States, the three carrier (AT&T, T-Mobile and Verizon) network, Soft, plans to use the existing Discovery Card network as a starting base. It is expected that Soft will also handle Visa, MasterCard and American Express branded cards in order to grow acceptance rates. Apple is also moving with an NFC based Device network. Apple has hired a PayPal executive with mobile payment experience. They have also been reported as buying Boku, another mobile payment organization.

In Europe, Nokia, the Finnish international terminal/phone supplier has signed an agreement with Tania Solutions, a mobile and professional services organization. Other mobile payment players include: Monitise, a UK based mobile payment service has a five year agreement with Visa. VIVOtech provides contactless and NFC mobile payments in Europe. Bling works with 15 midwestern USA banks. They use a sticker Device that provides network attachment to existing phones. They have partnered with PayPal.

Ixaris is a UK based company providing "Paylets", a mobile payment application. Their Opn platform also supports Visa, MasterCard and Swift (communications)

Network. XIPWIRE offers a PIN based money transfer application. XIPWIRE is a Pennsylvania, USA, based smart Device using payment service.

These represent the major mobile payment services in the world. There are probably others. Eventually, mutual standards will bring all the players into a compatible method of operation. Clearly we are heading towards a Smart Device based financial transaction world.

Bank Branches Will Continue as an Essential Marketing Venue

The branch offices of a financial institution will continue to be an important physical venue. It will be the scene for introducing customers to the new electronic and communications based transaction bank. It will continue to process the physical transactions for the very small percentage of customers unable to transit to the new Smart Device communications based process.

The marketing branch will be the location to establish the customer's "Personal Profile". In an electronic bank, there will not be a teller present during the payment transaction to understand the customer present and to react appropriately. The new source of that information will be a previously compiled set of data to be known as the "Personal Profile". What language does the customer speak? What account types does the customer have and understand. ? Can the customer read and write ? Do the displayed characters have to be enlarged to accommodate the customer's eyesight level ? These and similar personal traits need to be recorded and responded to by the serving system, when a teller is not involved to assess the customer during the transaction. This will also allow improving the responses of self-service units to specific customers' interface needs. The disappearing element will be the physical transaction with face-to-face customer-teller action.

Options Internet Based Marketing Will Add to Bank Marketing

A critical continuing need in any bank is the marketing of new and additional bank products to clients and prospects. The development of Smart Device based marketing will follow from the major development of Internet based retail merchandizing. The substantial growth of Internet based retailing demonstrates the well established Internet based techniques for communicating product and services availability and benefits.

These need to be followed with the appropriate payment and delivery methodology. "Internet Retailing" is well established and offers marketing options that will reach bank customers with timely product offerings. The marketing options will be available 24/7 via the Internet. The options will be supported with a variety of techniques ranging from TV equivalent commercials to step-by-step explorations of the banking product advantages and potential results. Furthermore, the availability of Internet based planning models and graphic displays will further enhance the offering of an expanding variety of Internet based financial packages and products.

Internet Industry Solutions:

Many of the concepts and processes that will be described for Smart Device based, Internet based, banking are also applicable to other industries. Retail, health care, and others industry applications will use these same type of techniques and processes. It is like the magnetic striped credit card. It was originally designed for use with banking and airlines. They are now use with every industry, world wide. More on these other industry electronic Internet usage opportunities later.

The Digital banking Business:

Migration to a Smart Device based, all electronic banking concept will have significant impact on conventional banking facilities. It will impact the physical attributes of the branch. Tellers for transaction processing will disappear as they are replaced by remote self service. It will significantly impact the roll of branch banking personnel. It will significantly reduce physical efforts such as mail delivery and processing. It will replace physical money and check security needs with network/ electronic based security functions and strategies. Visits to the "branch" will be accomplished electronically. The business of electronic banking will be 24/7. Successful bankers will need to move rapidly to keep up with the rapidly changing, remote, electronic functional, Smart Device environment.

An all electronic, Smart Device based banking environment offers significant improvements in delivering bank products. It will offer faster delivery to most remote transaction locations. It will exercise better controls.

Surviving as an Internet Banker:

One last observation before the details. You will read about many new concepts associated with the Internet based, Smart Device based, banking environment. Understanding and applying them is not an option. The most desirable set of bank customers—the young and Internet Industry Solutions:

Many of the concepts and processes that will be described for Smart Device based, Internet based, banking are also applicable to other industries. Retail, health care, and others industry applications will use these same type of techniques and processes. It is like the magnetic striped credit card. It was originally designed for use with banking and airlines. They are now use with every industry, world wide. More on these other industry electronic Internet usage opportunities later.

The Digital banking Business:

Migration to a Smart Device based, all electronic banking concept will have significant impact on conventional banking facilities. It will impact the physical attributes of the branch. Tellers for transaction processing will disappear as they are replaced by remote self service. It will significantly impact the roll of branch banking personnel. It will significantly reduce physical efforts such as mail delivery and processing. It will replace physical money and check security needs with network/ electronic based security functions and strategies. Visits to the "branch" will be accomplished electronically. The business of electronic banking will be 24/7. Successful bankers will need to move rapidly to keep up with the rapidly changing, remote, electronic functional, Smart Device environment.

An all electronic, Smart Device based banking environment offers significant improvements in delivering bank products. It will offer faster delivery to most remote transaction locations. It will exercise better controls. electronic game trained crowd—have the ability to rapidly to understand, accept and stay ahead of these concepts at a rate equal to that of your youngest and most aggressive market place customers.

Better Controls

Perhaps, more importantly, it will quickly identify new options and opportunities for using bank services and products. As the number of Internet based bank products increase, it will be essential for the banking systems to follow the customer's use of bank processes and to then make suggestions. The suggestions will be based on a customer's personal profile. More on the "Personal" Internet Industry Solutions:

An all electronic, Smart Device based banking environment offers significant improvements in delivering bank products. It will offer faster delivery to most remote transaction locations. It will exercise better controls. The electronic game trained crowd—have the ability to displayed words replacing printed words

An important byproduct of the migration to all electronic banking will be the replacement of the "printed" word with the "displayed" word. The shift to display based cell and Smart Devices reflects this change. The demise of the printed newspaper in the shift to electronic displays and the advent of the electronic book (e-books) demonstrates the acceptance of this shift to displayed information. In fact, the shift of society to television was an early and strong indicator of this transition. This shift will have a profound impact on industry implementation and the need for more and more information display bandwidth support. On the other hand, it will help a lot of paper-producing trees survive the growth of our civilizations.

How Rapid a Transition?

The changes described and projected in this text are already happening. The key question is how rapidly will the majority of the bank using population migrate to the paperless, all electronic, Internet based, mobile Device bank? That answer is a function of you and your customers. Today, more than 100 years after the introduction of the internal combustion engine, there is still a small segment of the population traveling by the earlier travel technology of the horse and buggy. Conversely, there is a segment of the population now reserving seats in high speed rocket assisted flights into orbital space and transcontinental flights.

The choice is yours. New technologies will offer you significant economic advantage by shifting to modern technologies and their improved performance for your customers. The banking industry has an excellent record of using technological progress to offer better and faster services. The goal of this report projection is to offer you a heads-up early indication of the events to happen in the banking industry. We wish you an insightful opportunity to avail your organization of these projected improvements, and their economic productivity.

The Bank Customer Will be an Important Bank Component

Smart Device based retail banking will benefit greatly from a prior decade of Smart Device usage and acceptance by the very important segment of new Smart Device users. By 2026 Smart Device usage will exceed 80% of the population. That included unbanked and under banked personnel conditioned to using Smart Devices for a variety of everyday purposes. The banking industry will undertake a massive education and promotion effort to show the Smart Device users the ease of migrating to Smart Device based banking transactions. An important requirement for that effort to succeed will be the economics of Smart Devices. Since customers will want the Smart Devices for purposes other than banking, an appropriate offer will be a partial payment incentive offered when a Smart Device based account is opened with a customer supplied Smart Device.

That incentive will be paid for by the bank's operational improvements from Smart Device usage. The bank's economic return will be discussed in more detail later. Needless to say, the added volume of Smart Devices required will incent manufacturers to achieve a better economy of scale.

And, now, on to the specifics.

Chapter i-2

What is a Smart Device ?

Purpose: To describe the Smart Device and examine its use.

Action: To provide a Smart Device selection basis.

Smart Device Evolution

The simple, hand held, portable telephone has evolved into a hand held computer, Internet based, and providing phone functions. It is the result of decades of electronic component functional growth and physical size reduction. The simple, hand-held, portable telephone has evolved to a compact, fist-sized, computer capable of 95% of the function of your desk top computer. Its portability reaches any place you can contact a network offering mobile Device electromagnetic signals. Its computational ability exercises any programmable computer application within the capability of its operational program system. In other words, the room full of computers in past decades now operate efficiently in your palm as a Smart Device. Furthermore, it has a full display, a keyboard, and communications interface.

Smart Device Acceptance

Recent executive surveys indicate that more than 80% of Smart Device using executives would reach for their Smart Device before their morning cup of coffee. Most executives (over 80%), would conduct business on their Smart Device before their desk phone. Family wise, their 8 years old children have already asked for their own Smart Device. You are likely to provide it to your 8 year old child for safety purposes, to allow their frequent family socializing and to provide instant access to their roaming. Some Smart Devices incorporate geographic positional sensing (GPS) to enable parents to quickly locate, physically, their children, to further enhance their Smart Device based safety. The built-in geographic position sensing has been used to very successfully track and locate lost and stolen Smart Devices.

Major Smart Device Component Parts

The Smart Device is a complete communications based computer system with a variety of input and output components. It is used to execute a variety of application programs intended to provide the user with specific set of banking related plans and results. Some of the applications are used for general financial results such as currency conversion, measurement conversions, and travel options. Other applications may be used for personal subjects of interest to the Smart Device owner. The major Smart Device components include:

A compact physical container/structure.
Protects components from weather and moisture.

Power supply—converts battery output to componentpower needs.

Power storage, e.g. a battery.

Display: Electronic and color with touch sensitivescreen. A variety of on-screen symbols for application and function identification andselection.

Communications interface and antenna

Digital, programmable computer

Wireless/contactless interface

Keyboards, function buttons and switches.

Microphone and speaker; Headset jack.

SIM card tray (defines communication/carrier protocol).

Manufacturer's labels

Other possible components:

Solar cells for power

Physical access key

Cover to protect antenna operation

Cord loop for carrying

Plastic card reading slot (stripe or contacts)

Finger grips

Battery access and cover.

Display light level control

Speaker/Headset volume control

Headset jack

Display scroll control

It is important to read the instructions provided by the manufacturer to identify all components and controls. Using the Smart Device, identify all components and controls. You should be able to identify and use them without looking at the unit. That degree of familiarity will assure your complete understanding of the unit you acquire and plan to use.

What is a Smart Device?

There are three types of hand held communications Devices.

The Personal Digital Assistant (PDA) has wireless capabilities. It uses Wi-Fi or Bluetooth. Wi-Fi is the trademark of the Wi-Fi Alliance of manufacturers providing wireless local area networks based on an IEEE 802.11 standard. Bluetooth is an open wireless technology for short distances created by Ericsson and managed by the Bluetooth Special Interest Group. The second type of hand held communications Device is the Smart Device (CP) which has PDA capabilities but communicates with cellular communications facilities. The third type is the Smart Device (SP) which is an Internet based, programmable computer, that has all the Smart Device (CP) communications capabilities.

There are two types of cellular networks. GSM (Global System for Mobile communications) is used by 80% of the global mobile market. It is used by more than 4.3 billion people across more than 212 countries. This digital technique is considered second generation (2G). CDMA (Code Division Multiple Access) uses a spread spectrum technique that allows multiple messages on the same channel. Phones intended to work on one network type do not generally work on the other.

Some network providers require you to purchase a matching phone from them. Ask before purchasing. It is possible to "Unlock" a phone. That allows the phone to work with any network. It is possible to buy an unlocking service to enable your phone to work with other networks. Most cellular providers subsidize the phone purchase price as a means to lock you into a multi-year contract. Hence, buying a phone from another source, a manufacturer or private party, may be more expensive. However, it allows you a more flexible arrangement in choosing or changing carriers. In fact, it allows you to buy prepaid amounts of communications, which is generally the least expensive arrangement.

Styles of Smart Devices.

Smart Devices are available in a variety of physical shapes and layouts. They generally differ in display and keyboard/data entry features. For each style, you can find GSM and CDMA network using units. The trick is to identify your desired carrier first, and then find a mobile Device to match your interface needs and operating requirements.

These Smart Devices May Use A Stylus (Touchscreen)

Traditional Style:

This type of phone style generally has a large screen which provides text entry using an on-screen, software based, keypad. This operation is generally supported by the use of Wndows Mobile software. It's disadvantage is that it may be a bit awkward to use as a smart Device. You may wish to use a headset for better phone communication. Try it !

Thumbpad Style

This style offers a square screen on top of an almost equal size thumb pad type keyboard. It does not offer an on-screen key board even though it has a touch screen for interaction. It works well as a smart Device and generally doe not require headset use. Its smaller screen shows less information. Its thumb pad keyboard may be difficult to use or to dial numbers for operators with large hands. Try it !

Slider Style:

The screen strongly resembles the "Traditional" PDA. The screens are generally smaller which makes the better for use as a phone. The keyboard is retracted and hidden when used as a phone. The full QWERTY keyboard is revealed by sliding it out. When slid out the image on the screen changes automatically from "portrait" to "landscape". Most cellular providers have a version of this phone. It is similar to the "Traditional" PDA. It's software is usually compatible. The keyboard is larger than the "Thumb pad". The "Slide" works well as a phone. There is a large selection of useful Windows Mobile software. The slider can be boxy. Not all application programs support both portrait and landscape display modes.

iPad Style

This is a large surface touch screen. The screen is occupied with the logo for each application program acquired. The screen also may be scrolled with finger movement to get to applications beyond the initial screen capacity. The unit is a handy smart Device size. Care must be taken not to damage the screen. The screen also needs to be cleaned from many finger marks accumulated in its use. The user needs to memorize the meaning of the content for each logo. Since there are more than 100,000 application candidates, that memorization can be challenging.

The Following Smart Devices Do Not Use A Stylus

Thumb Pad Style

Microsoft calls these units Smart Devices. All software actions are done by hardware buttons. This phone has been popular because these units are very compact and slim. Operation is geared to a one handed usage. The display is not a touch screen. Software must be written for a non touch Device and those programs are more limited. The thumb pad works well as a phone. However, the lack of a touch screen may be considered awkward by some users. People with large fingers may have trouble dialing numbers and the software may be limited. Try it !

Flip Phone Style:

This is a "Clamshell" type phone. Text entry is time consuming as it uses a "T9" text entry. This method of text entry requires multiple key strokes for each character. This unit does not have a touch screen. Hence, software is more limited. Touch screen software will not work on this style smart Device. The unit has an excellent shape for use as a phone. However, the text entry without a touch screen can be very time consuming. A small screen and limited software may make this unit difficult to use.

Candy Bar Style

This is a less common smart Device style. It uses the time consuming "T9" multiple key entry per character. It lacks a touch screen and software is generally limited. However, it has an excellent shape for phone use. Lack of a touch screen and limited software make this unit difficult to use.

Picking a Smart Device

Consider these three factors, in this order:

1): The Carrier: do they provide the geographic coverage, communications features and the economic alternatives you require ?

2): The Smart Device or Smart Device features and functions: Does the unit have display, interactive functions and the features you need ?

3): The Software: Do the functions and features match your phone characteristics (e.g. touch screen vs key entry). Does the software also offer the growth of functions and applications you may need later, such as navigating, messaging, multi-media, and service support.

Buying a Smart Device

Smart Devices are becoming more complex and more like mini computers. What counts is what goes on inside of them. Consider the basic features:

The Processor: Phone performance is dependent on processor speed. The faster, the better. High end Smart Devices generally come equipped with a 1 GHZ processor.

2) The RAM: The more Random Access Memory capacity, the better able the Smart Device to do multi-tasking. High-end phones have at least 512 MB of RAM.

3) The Display Screen: There are two important types of touch screens—Resistive and Capacitive. The Capacitive is considered faster and responds to human touch. The Resistive screen can be used with Devices like a stylus.

The OLED and AMOLED screens give strong color with amazing brightness when used indoors but fade when used indoors. Super AMOLED has fixed that problem. AMOLED is also good for watching TV. TFTLCD screens have an inadequate viewing angle, present faded blacks, and low brightness levels. A screen size of 3.2 to 3.5 inches is the best viewing size and is easily carried in pockets and purses.

4) Check the keyboard: These are a personal, preference, whether real or virtual. Do you touch type or hunt and peck? Do you need tactile feedback from a key depression ?

5) The platform and application software: Which applications best suit your needs ? Check the software options and usage before making a final decision.

The Smart Device Usage Challenges

There are two sets of challenges with Smart Devices. One set relates to your selection and use of a pocket computer interfacing a variety of communication alternatives. Included are:

Smart Device selection and usage training Smart Device economics.
Smart Devices rules and policies—employer and employee.
Care and feeding of a sophisticated electronic
Device e.g SIM card and battery change Control and maintenance of the Smart Device.
Transition to later models.

The other set of challenges relate to managing a number of Smart Devices interconnected to a business organization, including:

Application development and evolution
"Unlocking" units to accept other networks applications "Jail Breaking" to switch communications networks.
Communications support and evolution
Maintenance and service
Cost of operation and usage
Employee units and customer units
Device and network management
Employee training and monitoring
Managing upagerading and evolution
Privacy and security requirements

Smart Device Operation

Your interface to the Smart Device are your eyes and fingers.

Your eyes identify icons on the screen, locate action buttons or screen touch points. Your eyes read messages, symbols and labels. With the large number of Smart Devices available, there are several alternatives actions possible to achieve a given operation on a Smart Device. For example, in one case a rotating knob will be a volume control. In another Smart Device, a touch sensitive moving marker on the screen may produce the same volume control result. These two Devices give equivalent operation. You must discover the mechanism used in the Smart Device you are handling.

(Internet reference: (/2007/09/26smart-primerN/) where N maybe 1, 2 or 3.

Chapter i-3

Smart Device Functions and Features

Purpose: Describe available Smart Device options.

Action: Choose the Smart Device functions you require.

Smart Device Operating Systems

An Operating System is a software program that runs on a computer and manages the computer components. It provides common services needed for efficient execution of application software. With application functions such as input, output, and memory allocation, the operating system acts as an intermediary between the application program (software) and the computer hardware.

The major Smart Device operating systems for Mobile Web and application usage in the United States (2/2016) are:

Android	33% Google Developed
RIM	29% Blackberry and Verizon
Apple	25%
Windows	8% Mobile
Palm	3% Also called Garnet Operating System

Other 2%

Radio-Frequency Identification Devices (RFID)

Radio-Frequency identification Devices (RFID) use an antenna to receive a radio signal carrying data and, possibly, electric power.

The signal is processed by an integrated circuit Device. The received signal identifies the source and inquires of the integrated circuit identification. The response is transmitted back via the antenna to the remote inquiry unit. In some cases, the received signal may also include power to energize the RFID unit. In other examples, the RFID unit may include a battery for power. There are a broad array of applications for RFID tags from automatic toll systems, to banking data capture and access control and security identification. RFID-like function may be added to existing smart Devices with a "sticker" carried RFID circuit.

The Changing Smart Device Spectrum: Tablets

As with any fast growing technology product area, the Smart Device is inviting the development of product variations and improvements. A good example is the development of "Tablet" Devices which include Smart Device functions. The tablet is a middle ground between the handheld Smart Device and the laptop computer. It has a 10 inch (diagonal) screen with "Touch Screen" response. The tablet allows a set of applications whose parameters exceed the capacity of a Smart Device. This includes document display, e-Book display facility, writing and editing of documents, a "virtual" keyboard (displayed), and photograph viewing. In addition, it offers the normal variety of Smart Device applications. Some tablets offer conventional smart Device facility together with wireless access. The tablet is too large to fit in a shirt pocket. It usually does fit in a coat pocket. Migration to a tablet size Smart Device opens several new Device applications, as follows:

> TV Content: The added display area permits viewing of TV formatted information. This may be pay TV or free TV, depending on the material source.

e-Book: The screen size allows displaying full size book pages. It has much of the look and feel of print on paper. E-Books in the United States vary, as follows:

Prices: From $ 79 to $ 489 (Amazon Kindle).

Screens: From 6 inches to 9.7 inches (Kindle).

Downloads: US 3G, Wi-Fi, and International 3G

Available books: Google (over 1 million), to Amazon (over 360,000).

Touch technology: Two types are available. A multilayer Resistive technology and a Capacitive technology using human body's electrical characteristics.

Some people prefer physical books. It is yours forever. You can access a book any time you want. Some e-Book providers limit the number of times you can down load an e-book content. The best resolution is to down load the e-Book content to your Personal Computer (PC). When you want to read the e-Book content transfer the e-Book content via USB connection to any e-Book of your choice. That will only work for Amazon's Kindle.

You can access thousands of e-Book contents from Project Guttenberg (pcworld.com/63480). This is a collaborative project of the University of North Carolina. It covers a broad array of information types, including software, music, literature, art, history and science. The content of Project Guttenberg is also visible on your Smart Device, not just Kindle. Feedbooks (feedbooks.com) is another good source of e-Book content. If the content is not Kindle compatible, you can convert the contents with Calibre (find. pcworld.com/63479). This program can also be used to manage your library content and synchronize your books content.

iPads to Replace Laptops

Access to internal corporate programs with iPad use is available with a free application program from Citrix Systems, Inc. The iPad also runs the same software as the iPhone with a number of business-friendly applications.

The iPads, with list prices of $ 429 to $ 829 are less expensive than laptop computers. In addition, the iPads provide better demonstrations, start more quickly and have longer lasting batteries. Their Pads have performed well with industry

Specialized applications. They have performed well in medical applications for viewing medical images such as X-Rays and CT Scans. The iPads are also better for accessing medical records. iPads have been used in hotels by concierges because of their ease in mobile use. The iPads have given construction managers mobile access to construction drawings and related support materials in the field.

Near Field Communication (NFC)

Near Field Communication (NFC), is a short range, high frequency, wireless communications technology. It enables the exchange of data between Devices which are up to four inches (10 centimeters) apart. The technology is a simple extension of the ISO/IEC 14443 proximity-card standard. It is used with contactless Devices in public transportation, payment and in mobile Devices. It communicates via magnetic field induction, where two loop antennas are within each other's field. This effectively forms an air-core transformer. NFC Devices are able to receive and transmit datat the same time.

NFC-enabled mobile Devices allow businesses to connect with consumers in new ways. By using the mobile wallet application, manufacturers and retailers can now send a coupon directly to the electronic wallet to influence the consumer's buying decisions, which is then tracked when the consumer uses the coupon.

Growth of NFC Usage

A Gartner report found that NFC will account for 30% of transaction volume worldwide in 2014, but only 5% in global transaction value. That indicates that NFC will, initially, be used for small transactions and for transportation tickets. There are several ways to implement NFC, including stickers, chips and smartcards. Bankers' plans are not yet clear for the choice with mobile Device payments. IMS Research forecasts that NFC IC chips will reach 785 million annually by 2015. An Israeli firm, Accells, has developed technology that allows any GSM Smart Device, world wide, to be used as a NFC Device, at low cost. It is expected to be used in India. (Ref: Payments Card and Mobile, July/August 2009, Page 26).

NFC Payments

Visand Nokiare also implementing NFC based payment Devices. (Ref: Payments, Card and Mobile, May/June 2009, Page 42). MasterCard is using an alternative NFC technology, M/Chip in its EMV card. (Ref: Payments, Card and Mobile, November/December 2009, Page 36). The GSM Association has called for NFC functionality to be built in from mid-2009. (Ref: Payments, Card and Mobile, January/February 2009, Page 16). The GSM Association uses the Single Wire Protocol (SWP), approved by the European Telecommunications Standards Institute (ETSI). The standard provides for an interface between SIM cards and NFC chip sets in a Smart Device. (Ref: Payment, Card and Mobile. January/February 2009, Page 16).

Adding Near Field Communications (NFC) Function

MasterCard has tested a Device produced by the Gemalto Company with most mobile Devices. You can see the physical Device "Upteq N-Flex" at (nfctimes/MasterCard-announces-future). The MasterCard test was with the DBS Bank, network operator StarHub, and EZLINK, operator of a contactless stored value card with more than 20,000 acceptance points in Singapore. The test and system had full government approval.

Eventually, all mobile Devices will have the NFC function built-in. These interim Devices are clearly a transitional step to provide a much needed function. The function is needed for mobile Devices without the NFC function.

Bar Code Scanning

Bar codes have been an effective form of quick data capture in retail transactions for forty years. Their function is now available using the optical capture properties of smart Device based cameras. The QR (Quick Response) optical code is an inch square configuration. It appears on printed advertisements. Using a QR interpreting application allows the smart Device to convert a picture of the QR configuration into a direct web page address (a URL). When used with an Internet browser, a QR scan and application delivers a URL based image to the mobile Device. This bypasses the need for searching and/or URL manual entry.

There are a wide variety of tools available to generate, read, and interpret QR high density bar codes. Google any of the following texts to obtain these QR code based application programs and tools:

QR Code Reader Software:

I-Nigma: Most popular decoder/reader application.

Optiscan: Best QR code scanner for i-Phones

QuickMark: for Windows Mobile and Symbian

Kaywa Reader

Jaxo Systems: for Java-enabled phones.

Active Print: Nokia series 60 camera phone only.

Nokia Reader: Nokia N80 series, plus a few N90's.

Google Zxing: Android and iPhone + others but not

Windows Mobile Devices.

SnapMaze: Nokia, Sony Ericson and Motorola phones

Red Laser: iPhone scanner for old style ID codes NeoReader:
For a good range of mobile Devices.

QR Code Software and Applications:

Bar Capture: Capture and decode QR from screens.

Online Decoder: Decode QR codes via image file URL

Wordpress QR Code Plug-in

InDesign C53 QR Code Plug-in

Firefox Mobile Barcode Add-on

Facebook QR Codes application

QR-Code Tag: Google Chrome QR Code Plug-in

A related mobile Device (Apple and Android Smart Devices) application
is Pricegrabber.com. Following the bar code scan, the result is processed
by pricegrabber.com application to find the lowest priced similar offering
on the Internet. This is a very handy information and comparison price
source when shopping with bar code scanning.

The SIM Card

The Subscriber Identification Module (SIM) stores the subscriber's
carrier data. The SIM card is issued by a carrier. The SIM card activates
any mobile Device into which it is inserted. However, the logical circuits
of the smart Device may allow the phone to be used on a specific carrier.
This is called a "locked" phone. There is a process whereby a smart
Device may be "unlocked". That allows the smart Device to work with

any carrier. The SIM card is then used for smart Device identification on the selected carrier.

An unlocked smart Device gives the user the ability to move the SIM card to another smart Device without signing a carrier contract. This also changes when a smart Device is damaged or if you want to change to an upageraded unit. Unlocked units are generally sold by the manufacturers and do not have carrier based modifications. Unlocked smart Devices can be migrated to foreign carriers with purchase of a local SIM card. That allows paying for calls with local charges.

3G / 4G Transmission Specifications

(Ref: HTC-EVO-4g-specs)

3G transmission has a basic download speed of up to 3.1 Mbps; Peak upload speeds of 1.8 Mbps; average download speeds of 600 Kbps to 1.4 Mbps.

4G transmission has a basic download speed of up to 10 Mbps; peak upload speeds of 1.0 Mbps; average download speeds of 3.0 to 6.0 Mbps.

HTC EVO Specifications

Processor:	1 GHZ ARM
Graphics:	Adreno 200: 22 M Triangles/second
Operating Sys:	Android 2.1
Memory:	512 MB
Storage:	1 GB Internal Display: 4.3" Trans. Reflective
Cellular:	4G Wi Max; 3G Edge
GPS:	Internal Digital Compass
WiFi:	802.11 b/g/n
Bluetooth:	V 2.1 + EDC

Front Facing Cam 1280x720 pel, 30 f/s

Camera:	8 mp auto focus, 720 p@30 f/s
Video Out:	Mini HDMI 1.4, 720 p
Battery:	1500 mah
Size:	4.8x2.6x0.5 inch
	Weight 6 oz/ 170 g
PHONE Cost:	$ 300 (with $ 100 mail in)
Call Plan:	$ 79.99 Sprint, 450 min
	Unlimited data, text
Assessment:	Best Wireless speed & Video chat
	Great media performance
	Google Mobile Services,
	Tactile Feedback Display

The iPhone (Ref: apple.com/iPhone/specs)

The iPhone is an iPad style Smart Device. It has a rich list of features and functions, including:

Processor:	1 GHZ ARM
Graphics:	Power VR 28 M Triangles/Second
Operating System:	Apple iPhone 4 Operating System
	System 7 and Mac OS Interface
Memory:	512 M B
Storage:	16/32 GB Internal
Display:	3.5 inch LCD, 326 p/in
Cellular:	3.5 HSDPA, 3 G Edge
GPS:	Internal Digital Compass
WiFi:	802.11 b/g/h
Bluetooth:	V2.1 + EDR
Front Face Camera:	640x480 p, 30 F/s

Camera:	640/480 p, VGA
Video Out:	1024X768 w/Doc
	576x400p w/Cable
Battery:	1420 mah
Size:	4.5x2.3x0.37 inch
Weight:	4.8 oz/136 g
Phone Cost:	$ 199 (16 GB), $ 299 (32 GB)
Call Plan:	$ 84 AT&T, 450 min
Assessment:	Best display w/video chat
	More Than 450,000 applications
	Ambient Light Control

Apple iPad For Comparison

The Apple iPad is a Device whose functions are between those of a Smart Device and a lap top unit. Its specifications are included here to show the common elements with a Smart Device. Also, to show its elements which are different from those of a Smart Device. Compare these specifications with those of the Apple iPhone 4, above.

Processor:	1 GHZ ARM
Graphics:	Power VR 28 M triangles/sec
Memory:	256 M Bytes
Storage:	16/32/64 G B
Display:	9.7 inch LCD
Cellular:	3.5 G HSDPA, 3 G Edge
	GPS Internal Digital Compass
Front Face Camera:	None
Camera:	None
Video Out:	1024x768 w/Dock
	576x400 p w/Cable

Battery:	6750 mah
Size:	9.6x7.5x0.5 inches
Weight:	25.6 oz, 730 g
Phone Cost:	$ 499 (16 GB)
	$ 629 (16 GB + 3G)

Smart Device Displays:

This is a rather complex subject, with changing technologies. To provide an up to date evaluation, use this URL to tap the latest evaluations available. (consumersearch.com/cell-phones/best-smart Devices).

The Anatomy of a Smart Device

Examining the major components of a Smart Device provides a guide to the major parts of a sophisticated computer system. industry Smart Device units (courtesy of the research firm iSuppli).

The Result

It is quite remarkable that the major components are so compact. Also, that the components have been engineered into a compact frame, with very high physical resistance to the physical abuse given to small, hand held units. Missing from the cost analysis are the application programs and operating systems needed to make the units perform useful results. The application program produces the required programming job results. The operating system causes the major components to work in a coordinated manner. Also missing is the information about the communications carrier performance and costs, vital for Smart Device application job results and performance economics.

Credit Card on a Phone

The Smart Device uses NFC capability to communicate with a transaction acceptor. The Smart Device is brought within 4 inches (or 10 centimeters) of the acceptor. This is equivalent to swiping a magnetic striped transaction card through a card slot reader. To enable this transaction, the Smart

Device contained application is opened with keying in a pin or a biometric read personal identification number. The application allows loading the equivalent of multiple account information within one Smart Device. This multiple account facility is used now in Southeast Asia countries. The NFC function allows two way communication. However, payment transactions are one way with account number going to the acceptor. Visa has tested this function in the United States and Southeast Asia.

Blackberry Smart Devices

There are a few dozen Blackberry Smart Devices. There are continuing announcements. A very useful comparison program for Blackberry Smart Devices is: (blackberry.com/eng/Devices/compare). For comparison purposes, the following is a list of specifications for a "Blackberry Bold 9700" Smart Device:

Processor:	624 MHZ Marvell
Graphics:	None
Memory:	256 MB
Storage:	1 GB Internal
Display:	2.44 inch LCD, 480x360 p
	Cellular 3.5 G HSDPA, 3 G EV-DO
GPS:	Internal Digital Compass
WiFi:	802.11 b/g
Bluetooth:	V2.1 + EDR
Front facing camera:	None
Camera:	3.2 MP Autofocus, 480x312 p, 30 f/s
Video Out:	None
Battery:	1550 mah
Size:	4.3x2.56x0.56 inch
Weight:	4.3 oz/122 g
Phone Cost: Call plan:	$ 199 (T Mobile).
Best:	Business and International Phone

Virtual Keyboards

A Virtual Keyboard is a keyboard projected onto a flat display. Keying is detected by a touch sensitive screen. Typing on a Virtual Keyboard is generally faster. It is not necessary to raise the finger tips between character strokes. Most Smart Devices will change the keyboard orientation by 90 degrees as the unit is rotated. This provides a horizontal virtual keyboard. Virtual keyboards also allow a function called Swype. That allows the fingertips to move across the virtual image without activating the virtual key stroke. Try it !

Access to "Jail breaking" and "Unlocking".

The Smart Device has a programmable computer. As such, they may be preprogrammed so as to be restricted to a specific network or to application programs which are operational only on a specific type of Smart Device. There are processes to break these prohibitions. "Jail Breaking" is the process which changes Smart Device programs to allow execution of previously prohibited programs. This practice has been supported by the Copyright Office of the Library of Congress.

"Unlocking" is the process of removing a Smart Device program prohibition of network attachment. Smart Device vendors enter into such an arrangement on a contractual basis to give one network a marketing advantage. Fortunately, the Smart Device purchaser who objects to that arrangement can obtain the "Unlocking" process. The process bypasses the prohibiting program.

3D (Three Dimensional) Displays

Using MeeGo, an open source software platform, Intel and Nokiare developing a smart Device display providing three dimensional images. The software will be useful on all mobile Devices from phones and tablets to television displays, automotive information and entertainment systems. The 3D displays are expected to give the user greater visual involvement. Check for the latest status when you want to proceed.

Solar Powered Mobile Devices

Several countries lack electrical energy generating facilities. Also, there may be times when a Smart Device battery can not be recharged. In both cases, the ability of a Smart Device to generate its own power is a necessary function. Several Smart Devices are available with an option for built-in solar cells. Smart Device usage needs to be in a geographic area with sufficient hours of sunshine to properly charge the Smart Device battery. Out of sunlight environment, e.g. in doors or underground, will need to have access to sunlight when needed. Likewise, the solar cells' surface will need to be cleaned for proper operation.

TV Programs Available on Smart Devices

"hulu" is a popular web-site offering TV shows. The web-site is free and offers access to TV shows on several major TC networks. Several Smart Devices offer the ability to view the TV shows. The application gaining access does charge a monthly fee. There is no reduction in the TV based advertisements. Some users object to paying for this Smart Device application and still having to view the ads.

There is a wide variation of Smart Device screen sizes, display densities, and related software functions. Also, there are different TV broadcast standards. The Smart Device user will have to test the TV application on their unit to ensure that it is capable of delivering an acceptable TV broadcast.

Motorola's DROIT X

The Droit X is an iPad style Smart Device. It uses Android, a mobile platform developed by Google. Its development was continued by the Open Handset Alliance.Its software is based on the Linux Operating System. Applications are written using the Java language. An Android software and application development kit is available from Google. The Android Smart Device has these specifications:

Processor:	1 GHZ ARM
Graphics:	Power VR, 14 M Triangles/Sec
Memory:	512 MB
Storage:	16/32 GB MicroSD
Display:	4.3 inch LCD, 854x480 p
Cellular:	3.5 G EVDO
GPS:	Internal Digital Compass
WiFi:	802.11b(11 Mb/s), g(54 Mb/s), n(200 Mb/s)
Bluetooth:	V2.1+EDR
Front Facing Camera:	None
Camera:	8 MP Auto focus, 720p @ 30f/s
Video Out:	None
Battery:	1570 and 1930 mah
Size:	5.0x2.6x0.4 inch
Weight:	5.6 oz, 158 g
Phone cost:	$ 199 Verizon
Call Plan:	$ 89.98, 40 min, unlmtd data, text.
Conclusion:	Great display, battery life, media output All specifications from: 5575317/smart Device-comparison-chart.

Conclusion:

Smart Devices are a fast growing product category with a large number of available products. Understanding the product options will provide you with a better opportunity to get the best Smart Device for your requirements.

Chapter i-4

Smart Device Operations

Purpose: Describe Smart Device Operation Options

Action: Select Smart Device Operational Options.

Making A Smart Device Call

A conventional phone call is a very simple process. The conventional phone is connected to a carrier. The line carries a dial tone 24/7. Lift the handset. Hear the dial tone. Enter the phone number you are calling. Listen for the dial signal change. If there is a ringing signal, wait for a response. If the called number is busy, hang up, and start over.

A Smart Device (or mobile Device) has several calling alternatives. The Smart Device does not have a dial tone. Rather, the number to be called is entered and the Send button, physical or virtual, is depressed. A visual indicator shows that the call has been initiated. The number to be called may be obtained from several sources within the Smart Device. These sources include:

> Frequent called numbers list.
> Respond to prior message content.
> Find the number with an Internet search.
>
> Use the last number called and captured.
> Use diary or calendar entries.
> Key entered by the caller.
> Various data bases with search access.

In addition to a variety of sources for the number to be called, there are a variety of ways to enter the number to be called by the Smart Device. These include:

Tactile response keyboard.

Non tactile response membrane keyboard.

Touch screen with a "virtual" keyboard.

Touch screen with tactile feedback.

Pointer or stylus (e.g. mouse like) entry.

Voice recognition entry.

Select and Execute an Application Program

Access the application directory for descriptions, prices, capacity requirements for storage and execution, display logo, network attachment, and performance needs. The selected applications are downloaded to the Smart Device. An identifying logo is displayed for later selection and execution.

There are more than 450,000 Smart Device applications depending on the Smart Device you are using. To illustrate the range of applications, the following is a list of the "must-own" Smart Device applications, courtesy of PC World magazine. Smart Device applications for multiple platforms:

(Note: many of these will also run on your PC).

Evernote: allows creation of text, photo and audio notes. Price: Free.

Remember the Milk: many features for managing your tasks. Price: Free.

Google Voice: provides a phone number to use for outgoing calls. Also, forwards calls to any phone. Price: Free.

Vlingo: replaces every instant where you must type voice commands. Price: Basic Free, Premium price varies by platform and version.

Personal Assistant: Tracks credit card transactions bank account status, and frequent flyer miles accounts. Price: Basic Free, $ 7 premium version.

LastPass: Manages your passwords. Price: $12 annual subscription.

Jott Assistant: Voice activated dictation. Price: $ 3 per month basic; $ 13 per month premium version.

ZumoDrive: Web based storage (also known as Cloud computing). Price: Free.

OurGroceries: Writes transferable grocery lists. Price: Free.

Craigsphone: Posts entries for your GPS identified location for Graigs list. Price: Free.

Dropbox: Allows sharing folders across all your computers. Price: Free.

Bump: Allows two Smart Devices to share data and bookmarks by physically bumbing. Price:Free.

CamCard: Scans and captures business cards. Price: $ 10 on Android, $ 7 on Apple.

NPR News: Receive NPR news through your Smart Device. Price: Free.

CNN Money: Real time financial reporting with a customizable format: Price: Free.

WeatherBug: detailed weather data. Price: Free.

Onion News Network: Access to Onion Network. Price: Free.

AP Mobile: Customize news with local reports. Price: Free.

MLB.com: Audio stream of major baseball news and scores: Price: $ 15.

Pixelpipe Post & Upload Pro: Time-saving way to reach all social networks: Price: Free.

Hootsuite: Manage social network user interface. Price: Free.

Foursquare: Reach other members and earn badges. Price: Free.

Layer Realty Browser: Overlay information about subjects within view. Price: Free.

Relief Central: Access to the CIA World Fact Book. Price: Free.

Mint: Provides real time financial management. Price: Free.

iStockManager: Access to and control of your TD Ameritrade Account. Price: Free.

Expensify: Creating and reporting expenses. Price: Free.

WorldMate: Access to world wide travel information. Price: Basic—Free; Premium— $ 12 per month.

Currency: Conversion of 180 different currencies. Price: Free.

SmrtGuard: Remotely track and lock a missing Smart Device. Price: Basic Free; Premium $ 5 per month.

Beejive IM: Allows chats with multiple networks. $ 10 for single Device. $ 15 for transferable license.

ItookThisOnMyPhone: Uploading picture and video to sharing sites. Price: Free.

RunKeeper: Uses Smart Device GPS to record your jogs. Price: Free.

Kindle: Use Smart Device to preview books. Price: Free.

Pandora: Streams your musinc preferences.

Price: Free.

Slacker: Pandora-like service with music stream capture for replay outside smart Device signal areas. Price: Free plus some features subscriptions.

Shazam: Identifies song name and artist. Price: Free.

MOG: A music service where you specify the songs or artist. Price: Free app plus $ 10 per month for service.

Thumbplay: Allows your music play list with on and off line listening. Price: $ 10 per month

Grooveshark: Find and stream a wide array of music sources with your own play lists. Price: $ 3 per month.

Slingplayer Mobile: Streams video from your cable box and DVR to your Smart Device. Price: $ 30.

Google Maps: Find business and travel directions. Price: Free.

Google Earth: Provides world wide satellite access with access to Wikipediand articles. Price: Free.

MapQuest 4 Mobile: Provides turn-by-turn directions and navigation. Price: Free.

Telenav: Provides turn-by-turn navagation to more than 10 million reviewed businesses. Price: $ 10.

Angry Birds: A game to retrieve stolen eggs.

Price: $ 1.

Doodle Jump: A game to move through various obstacles. Price: $ 1.

Ookla: Checks wireless uploading and down loading speeds. Price: Free.

Applications for Android:

Toddler Lock: Turns Smart Device into colorful toy, touch sensitive and with soothing sounds. Price: Free.

Thinking Space: Provides "mind mapping" to organize and form new concepts. Price: Free with ad support, $ 4 premium version.

Astro File Manager: Makes Smart Device act as miniature PC. Price: Free with ad support, $ 4 premium version.

Missed Call: Customize visual and audio output for missed and incoming calls. Price: Free.

SkyFire: Browser with streaming video. Price: Free.

Dolphin Browser: A very functional browser. Price: Free.

Bookmarklet: Allowing sharing Web pages with social networks. Price: Free.

WIFI Analyzer: Finds least crowded Wi-Fi channel and shows strength. Price: Free.

Barcode Scanner: Handles all bar codes to obtain associated product or URL. Price: Free.

Gtasks: Works with Google Tasks and access Gmail and Google Calendar. Price: Free.

BeyondPod: Manages the Android music player with audio and video podcasts. Price: Basic Free, $ 7 premium.

Listen: Search audio feeds and integrate with Google Reader. Price: Free.

AntiDroid Theft: Turns on remote GPS tracking to find a lost Smart Device. Price: Free.

AndroZip File Manager: Works with and creates ZIPhone archives. Price: Free.

Gesture Search: lets you find files quickly. Price: Free.

Picase Toot Pro: Manages photographs and albums. Price: Free.

Smart Measure: Measures heights and distances. Price: Free.

Spirit Level Plus: Use Smart Device to show level and measure angles. Price: Free.

Color Flashlight: Converts Smart Device into multi color flashlight. Price: Free.

Digital Recipe Sidekick: Import recipes, save them on an SD Card, edit and email them. Price: Free.

Handcent SMS: Customizable texting tool. Price: Free.

ConvertMe: Currency converter and tip calculator. Price: Free.

Applications for the iPhone:

Line2: Adds a second line to your Smart Device. Price: $ 15 per month.

WolframAlpha: Answers questions in sentence form. Price: $ 2.

Atomic Browser: creates browser on iPhone screen. Price: Basic Free, Premium $ 1.

Last.FM: Plays music of desired artist. Price: Free.

Public Radio Tuner: Provides lists of local stations. Price: Free.

CalenGoo: Merges with your Google calendar and issues invitations. Price $ 7.

1Password: Stores your passwords and other personal information. Price: Basic $ 10, Premium $ 15.

Wi-Fi Finder: National directory of hotspots. Price: Free.

Instapaper: Saves Web articles browsed by your iPhone. Price: $ 5.

Whole Foods: Display recipes. Price: Free.

How To Cook Everything: Acess to 2,000 recipes and cooking advice. Price: $5.

Lose it: Keeping track of calorie intake.

Price: Free.

Tom Tom: Turns your Smart Device into a GPS Device. Price: $ 50.

IncrediBooth: Gives you an almost genuine photo-booth experience. Price: $ 1. Diptic: Combines photographs. Price: $ 2.

I Love Katamari: Follow a rolling highly adhesive ball. Price: $ 6.99.

Plants vs Zombies: Defending your home from an invasion of deadly flora. Price: $ 3.

Words with Friends: Scrabble like word game. Price: Free.

Applications for BlackBerry.

UberTwitter: Adds location, images and video to

Twitter. Price: Free.

Crunch SMS: Adds customization options to SMS applications. Price: Free.

BlackBerry Messenger: Chat and exchange information with other BlackBerries. Price: Free.

Nobex Radio Companion: Listen to radio stations in United States. Premium gives access to 5800 stations in 80 countries. Price: Free for USA, $ 4 for premium version.

PodTrapper Podcast Manager: Downloads podcasts and creates playlists. Price: $ 10.

BitBop: Streams premium TV to Smart Device.

Price: $ 10 per month.

Mobile Checkbook: Keeps complete personal financial records. Price: $ 10.

Viigo: delivers complete news reports. Price: Free.

Berry Weather: Complete weather reports. Price: $ 10.

Tether: Connects PC or Mac computer to the Internet through the BlackBerry 3G service. Price $ 50.

QuickLaunch: Setup unlimited shortcuts to any Websight, file or application. Price: $ 5.

BerryBuzz: Customize alert system to continue until acknowledged. Price: $ 6 per month.

These 100 Smart Device applications are a small sample of the more than 450,000 available for most vendor units. When selecting a unit, check the applications available for your potential purchase. Match them against your requirements. That will assure you of a maximum return on your Smart Device investment.

Image Capture and Use

Selecting image types and parameters, displaying and capturing images, editing images, processing images, using images in output and email. There are a variety of image based applications. Smart Device capture of a check images enables check processing and electronic depositing of funds. Smart Device image capture of a bar code or QR high density bar code enables conversion of the image to a URL for a search bypassing Internet access and a web page retrieval.

Message Processing and Transmission

Receiving, saving, editing and sending messages.

Network attachment and security functions.

Internet Access and Browsing

An Internet web page address (a URL) is entered in the browser and an access action is initiated. The response is the Web page addressed.

A search is initiated for a given argument or search description. The search responds with a series of potential Web page candidates. The user must then examine the search stream result for an appropriate response, with a given Web page URL included. The chosen response is then used to initiate an access.

A high density bar code such as the QR code is photographed by the Smart Device camera. The application program coverts the QR code into a URL. The URL is used to initiate a Web page access.

Monetary Value Capture and Payment

The Smart Device introduces several new techniques for value transfer. Smart Device to Smart Device transfers are achieved with the use of the Near Field Communications (NFC). These value transfers will occur between individuals, and with vendors or merchants. They will also occur through the Internet in a manner similar to withdrawing funds from a paperless ATM.

In a transition period, the Smart Device will be used to capture a check image (two sides). The check image will be communicated to a financial institution. There it be processed with an image capture system. The check amount will be interpreted by the processing program. The account will be credited to the deposit account. The check image will then be communicated by the processing system to the origination institution.

Bar Codes Access and Use

Bar codes are a dense information form. Using the Smart Device camera function, they may be captured for quick reading of URLs and then using them for Browser access to their designated Web page. To generate bar codes download quikqr.com or snappr.com. Download beetagg.com to scan a bar code, to move the resulting URL to the Smart Device browser and initiate display of the accessed Web page. The bar codes may be found on many printed sales offerings.

Appointment Capture, Scheduling and Response

The Smart Device provides a number of functions to achieve effective time management. Included are:

1) Receive eMail: establishes communicationswith major association contacts andmembers. Provides up to date reports ofstatus and events.

2) Keep an up to date calendar. Allowsadding events straight into the calendar.

3) Use Google to get the latest news byinterest categories.

4) Use bookmarks to capture pages of interest.

5) Access social media for possible entries.

Video Capture and Use

Securing Phone Operations and Data

Coordinating with PC's.

Chapter i-5

Introducing Your Smart Device

Purpose: To understand the operation of your Smart Device

Action: What to do after you open the box.

Familiarization (Based on the BlackBerry Smart Device).

Find the "On" button. It is generally in the lower right corner with a sun-like icon. It may also be a button in the upper left corner. When the button is depressed the screen becomes illuminated. The keyboard also becomes illuminated. Identify the speaker, microphone and earphone connection socket. On the reverse side find the removable cover for the battery and SIM card. The SIM card contains the information giving you access to a carrier and to a specific phone number. Moving the SIM card to another Smart Device gives it access to the identified phone number and carrier. Welcome to the world of thumb typing. Your thumbs enter information while the other fingers support the Smart Device.

Identify the track wheel. Moving the track wheel up and down changes the screen display. Depressing the track wheel selects or activates menus. Identify the keys which actuate other functions such as keyboard extension (The Alt Key), shift to capital characters (The Cap Key), begin and end Call keys, activate the browser (The Browser Key), and, sometimes, the Next Key which is equivalent to scrolling the track wheel up.

The initial home screen uses display icons to communicate Smart Device status, provide the current date and time and signal battery strength.

The prime screen content are application icons and icons for shortcuts to applications. (Each of the applications listed in Chapter I-4 "Smart Device Operations", would have an icon in the display which is a shortcut to activate the selected application). With application libraries exceeding 450,000 programs for most Smart Devices, it is necessary to select the handful you most frequently will use. Those are the applications with shortcut activation links initiated with the displayed icons.

Installing the Desktop Manager

The Desktop Manager is a program which supervises the flow of messages to your Smart Device. Its first task is to set up your Smart Device to receive messages. The next step is to launch the program to work with your email source to receive your incoming emails. Subsequent steps display themail content and let you take action to dispose of the item. Those include no action or discarding, or, storing for future reference, or preparing a response. Other actions include redirecting the mail to another party, or adding a comment and forwarding the modified message. All of these options are provided in the actions available with the Desktop Manager.

Customizing your Smart Device

There are many ways to personalize your Smart Device. Start by setting the time and date to be displayed. Use the track wheel to display the fields to be set. These include the hour, minute, month, day and year. Next, set up the ownership information including name, address, email address, and phone number. Another option is the sounds made by the unit in response to events. This may be a tone or vibration, or a combination of the two. The screen will offer display options of font types and sizes. These also need to be selected and set for personalization. Another option is the "screen saver" icon which is displayed with no actions after a specified period of time.Up grading the Software and Operating System

The Desktop Manager is used to install new software. The latest software is obtained from your carrier. Search the support web page of the carrier.

When found, the software is installed by the Desktop Manager. After installing the new software, launch the Desktop Manager and connect your Smart Device to the desktop PC. The Desktop Manager will notice the new version of software is available and will display a prompt asking if you would like to install the new software.

Installing new software is a complicated process. It will take several steps to get your Smart Device back to the same state where it was when you started. During the process your Smart Device will be WIPED CLEAN! Therefore, a complete backup and restore are essential parts of the process. Once started, the status of each step is displayed as it progresses through the upagerade. When done, take time to explore the new software.

Compiling and Sending Messages

This is the most used application. A message is more than an email. There are several types of messages:

* Short Message Service (SMS) are addressed to phone numbers. They are typically less than 150 characters.

* Phone call: It includes information about a placed or Email: These may be sent or received emails.

* PIN Message: Similar to email, but with higher priority. Includes information about delivery success.

Message preparation includes access to the Address Book. Contact information is saved for use one or more times. Following selection of the message type, a standard screen is displayed to facilitate message composition. This includes the "to field", added copies (cc:) and blind copies(bcc:). Blind copies are not disclosed to the other recipients. When the message is sent, a rotating icon indicates the process is underway. The icon will change after the message has been sent.

Received messages can be opened to read the content. Other options include "Forwarding" the message to another recipient. You may add the sender's identification to your address book. You may also add a note for later use, or you may delete the message from your receive file.

Received message may have a wide variety of attachments. Using the "open attachment" menu will display the attachment content. Longer attachments may be read in sections.

Internet Browsers

A "Browser" is a software program intended to search the web and retrieve a particular web address (URL) content. There are a variety of browsers. Who provides the browser ? You must know the source to assess its security. A browser from your carrier or prime software provider is probably very secure. A browser whose content goes through the security screen of your usual server is also reliable, especially if it is scanned by your security program which scans for possible viruses and other problem sources.

Once a web page is located by the browser, you will need to display the content. They you must interact with its options. You may need to create a reply message and send it to the provided address.

Bookmarks or Favorites

This browser provided function keeps track of your commonly visited web pages. A simple selection from the bookmark list avoids having to type a URL (web page address) for a desired web page access. This also avoids the need to select and use a search program. It also avoids the need to examine the lengthy output of a search program to find the desired web page. Adding a bookmark to the list requires the browser to capture the complete address (URL) of the required web page. Generally, the full web page address is not shown in the list. Sometimes a bookmark entry is not correct. That entry needs to be erased and recaptured to ensure correctness. Bookmarks can be moved within the list. This allows you to locate bookmarks in groups, or by access frequency. The bookmarks are one of the most important capabilities of a browser. Hence, when preparing to select and use a browser, the bookmark function should be carefully received and tested. Removing infrequently used bookmarks will be necessary to make room for more frequently used entries. This prevents running out of space for necessary bookmarks.

Phone Calls

The "Recently Called" list indicates the most recently called numbers. The list continues to automatically reorder entry sequence to reflect actual calling frequency. The list is very useful in placing calls without having to re-enter recently called numbers. You can also delete less frequently used numbers. Receiving calls displays the caller's number, if known. Other options include receiving multiple calls, creating a conference call by connecting two calls and muting your voice while listening to an incoming call. Other options include adding notes to a call history, call forwarding, call logging and call barring.

Address Books

This application simplifies placing calls by using previously captured calling information. The book entry can be captured during previous calls or may be entered by the key board. The book can also hold multiple telephone numbers for selected individuals. Individual entries can be edited or deleted if no longer required. Group entries are possible with multiple names using a single phone number. Individual address entries can be assigned to multiple categories.

Calendars

Entries are used to keep track of meetings, appointments, and important events. Entries can be established to automatically recur without additional input. Calendars offer four ways to view information. These are: 1) Monthly; 2) Weekly; 3) Daily; and 4) By agenda. The monthly view is similar to a wall calendar format with small boxes. The weekly view is marked but does not provide for entry. The daily view does offer a text description of the event. The calendar entries have a start, end and duration fields. A time zone entry will automatically adjust to your time zone. A "private" indication will hide appointment details from others. The "note" field allows you to enter additional text not visible to others. The "recurrence" field will automatically cause the event to reoccur, as indicated. All entries may be edited, deleted, or selectable display options exercise. That later includes the sequence of information display when the calendar is opened.

Tasks

The task application is a "to-do" list. However, it has several added options including status and due dates. The entries include a name, a due date, and a task status. Included are: not started, in progress, completed, waiting and deferred; and a priority indication. The task application allows finding a task, by name.

Other Applications in Your Smart Device

Memo pad: provides for a title and free-form entry.

Setting an alarm: Allows a date and time entry. You may select the type of notification to be used.

Calculator: Provides for a range of mathematical functions. It also allows selection of the English or Metric system of measurement. It also offers conversion between the two measurement systems.

Password keeper: Stores passwords and keeps usage records. It also can generate random passwords, needed. Password characters may be masked by replacing the individual characters in the password with stars or other symbols.

Finding and Installing Applications from Elsewhere

There are several sources of Smart Device applications. Included are: Handango.com, PDATopsoft.com and rimroad.com. There are many others. In addition, you may create your own applications. Check blackberry.com/developers/index.shtml. Use the Desktop Manager to install a new application.

Chapter i-6

Smart Device Problems and Fixes

Purpose: To identify Smart Device issues requiring your attention.

Action: Understand the issues and fixes before they are a problem.

Note:

The Smart Device industry has a constant flow of new Devices, platforms and applications. It will also be difficult to distinguish between personal and organization owned with a mixture of operating program systems functions and features. Try to select a vendor supporting a combination of Devices. Invest in integration and protection efforts to prepare for change and, especially, against unannounced attacks.

The Smart Device can be a very useful Device in an emergency. There are a number of functions available in all Smart Devices and Smart Devices for use when an emergency arises. Let's consider several.

Do You Need Smart Device Insurance ?

The recommendation in most cases is no ! An average cost in the United States has been found to be US$ 5.64 per month. In most cases you will be asked to sign a two year contract. That is more than $ 130 when the two year period is up. Did your unit cost that much ? If your unit cost more, check the warrantee. If damage is covered for the first year, why should you purchase insurance ? If you decide to buy insurance read the policy carefully. Most will not pay for damage caused by water or other events such as dropping. A lot of Smart Devices end up in toilets. Hence, the damage will not be covered.

Check your policy to see if there is a deductible for obtaining a new Smart Device. Another payment of $ 50 might be required to get a new Smart Device. A recent study showed an average Smart Device life of 18months. In most cases the units are replaced because they have become obsolete. Most insurance companies replace damaged units with a same or refurbished units. In either case you have an old model.

The Smart Device Emergency Number, Worldwide.

Entering the digits 1 1 2 gives access to the Smart Device or Smart Device network based Emergency Service. Entering this number will work when the keyboard is locked. It will also provide emergency access when you are outside the coverage area of your mobile network. Try it ! Try it to test its emergency availability, anywhere.

Opening Your Card Door Remotely.

You have locked your keys and door opener in you car. You do have your Smart Device. You call home where there is a duplicate door opener. You hold your Smart Device within 12 inches of you car door. The remote door opener is exercised next to the remote phone. The sound travels to your Smart Device at the car and the car door opens. There is no distance or weather limitation. Anywhere you can reach with your Smart Device or Smart Device you have access to another door opener. Try it to test this process for your card door opener and remote access. The same process works for any sound based opener, such as a car trunk access Device. This process will save you a call to a car emergency service. It will avoid having someone having to drive miles to bring you another set of keys to open your locked car.

Emergency Battery Power for Your Smart Device.

Most Smart Devices have a built-in emergency power reserve. When your Smart Device indicates a low cell battery power level, key in 3370#. This code will cause your Smart Device or Smart Device to restart using the built-in power reserve. The reserve power reserve will get recharged next time you charge your Smart Device or Smart Device. There is generally no indicator for this battery power reserve. Try it.

Finding A Misplaced Smart Device

If you are sure the Smart Device is nearby but can't locate it, call it from another phone or Smart Device. That will cause your Smart Device to ring until you can locate it. If you have lowered or turned off the ring volume, there are applications designed to change the current settings on your Smart Device. For Android users there is "Where's my Droid" (findpcworld. com/69855). This program lets you set up a password. Send the password by SMS email address. On receipt, the password automatically adjusts the Smart Device ring to maximum volume. The Smart Device rings for preset time period, or until you turn it off.

The BlackBerry program is (findpcworld.com/69858). The free application rings the unit. The $ 4 paid version provides a GPS location. iPhone has a $0.99 application called Beep My Cell (findpcworld. com/69858). This application triggers a beeping by logging into beepmycell.com. Google has a low cost utility (find.pcworld. com/69858). This $ 1.50 application kicks on the Smart Device ringer and transmits the Smart Device GPS location to the initiating Smart Device. This gives two ways to look for the misplaced Smart Device.

Creating a Smart Device Backup

Your Smart Device accumulates a good amount of data from your use. Cabling your Smart Device to a PC with Windows Mobile opens a synchronous utility that creates a complete backup of your Smart Device content. The Android application (findpcworld.com/69859) is a $5 application program which sends all phone related data to a secure server. If you can't find your Smart Device, you can download the stored Smart Device data to a replacement unit.

For permanently lost Smart Devices, TenCube's WaveSecure (findpcworld. com/69860) is available for most Smart Devices with a complete package of protection. WaveSecure lets you remotely back up the content of your phone to a secure server. When loaded it wipes out all of your data from the Smart Device. Apple offers a similar tracking service called Find My iPhone (find.pcworld.com/69861). It costs $ 99 per year.

Disabling A Lost or Stolen Smart Device or Smart Device

All Smart Devices and Smart Devices have an assigned identification number. The identification number is about 15 digits. You can see the identification number by keying *#06#. Copy the displayed identification number for future reference. When your phone is lost or stolen, call your carrier or service provider. Give them the identification number. Request them to block all calls from the Smart Device or Smart Device with that identification number.

Service providers are able to block calls from a phone with the designated identification number even if the SIM card is changed. The SIM card provides network access identification. This blockage action makes use of the Smart Device or Smart Device useless. However, you may not get your Smart Device or Smart Device returned. However, the phone can not be used or sold. Your action does avoid charges for further phone use or for additional calls.

Two other secret codes are used by Smart Device manufacturers. *#2820# displays your Smart Device's Bluetooth address. It is useful when setting up a wireless network, or when troubleshooting a Bluetooth network. Another code is *#0000# which shows the version number of your firmware. It is needed when discussing a phone repair.

Access Free Information Services with Your Phones.

Normally, phone companies charge for information (411) information requests. Smart Device companies provide a free information service that is very useful. The free service is very useful while you are away from your directories or telephone number list on your desk computer. To use the free smart Device or Smart Device information service enter 800 373 3411 (800 FREE 411). The voice answer back will offer you the equivalent of both white (alphabetic) and yellow (by category) page directory access. In addition, it will generally offer short games or horoscope options. It is all free. Try it.

Drying a Wet Smart Device

Accidents do happen ! Smart Devices fall into water. When they do, here are the suggested steps to take. 1) Remove the battery as soon as possible. 2) Remove the SIM card. 3) Pry open the unit (See "find. pcworld.com/63487" or 63488). 4) Remove all screws. Check under labels. 5) Wash out the unit. Place the unit in a container with dry rice.

Signal Boosters for Mobile Devices

Some geographic areas experience weaker communications signals, for a variety of reasons. These include terrain interference with line of sight transmission, building construction, and related signal blockage reasons. In these problem areas it is possible to employee a frequency selective amplifier to produce locally a stronger smart Device signal. The booster units come in a variety of configurations. They provide for: 1) Personal workspaces ($ 119-169); 2) Car ($ 299); 3) Home and office space to 2500 square feet with multiple user support ($ 299-399). Check with www.wi-ex.com or USA based 1-800 871 1612. These designs support most USA based carriers. (Ref: PC World, November 2008, page17).

Cutting costs of your smart Device bill.

> Reduce the cost of your plan by reducing the number of minutes to your actual needs. Check six months of bills to determine the actual number of minutes you have been using. Then switch plans to a more appropriate level.

> Use a family-plan for family calls, which are usually lower cost.

> Check the numbers being called. With a small number of frequently called numbers, change your calling plan.

If you do a lot of text messaging, consider buying a bundle of messages at a lower cost.

With an unusually large monthly bill, call the carrier to negotiate a lower charge that that period.

For transmission of a large amount of data, call the carrier for a large data tariff. Use available services to examine your bills for possible improvements. They are billshink.com and myvalidas.com.

Watch out for termination fees. Timing your departure may reduce this cost exposure.

(From ConsumerReports.org).

How Much Radiation do Smart Devices Emit ?

The SAR (specific absorption rate) is a value that Corresponds to the relative amount of radio frequency energy absorbed in the head of a user of a wireless Device. The FCC limit for public exposure from cellular telephones is an SAR level of 1.6 watts per kilogram of user weight. The SAR ratings of some typical phones are:

BlackBerry Bold 9700:	1.55 Wt/kg
Motorola Droid A855 phone:	1.5 Wt/kg
LG Chocalate Touch (VX8575):	1.46 Wt/kg
HTC Nexus One (Google):	1.39 Wt/kg
Apple iPhone (3GS):	1.19 Wt/kg

San Francisco has a "Smart Device Right-to-Know" Ordinance which requires retailers to include next to each phone the maximum amount of radiation that the model emits. The purpose of the ordinance is to allow a better informed buyer decision.

How do you reduce the risk of exposure to radiation from smart Devices?:

> Buy a low-radiation smart Device.
>
> Use a head set or speaker.
>
> Hold your phone away from your body.
>
> Use the phone as a speaker phone.
>
> Chose texting over talking.
>
> If you have a poor signal, stay off the phone.

(Ref: San Jose Mercury News, NY Times) A Danish study examining 358,403 cellphone users aged 30 and over, from 1990 to 2007, found users do not have a higher cancer risk compared to those without cellphones.(AP).

How to avoid too many Smart Device calls or Spam?

> There are some obvious fixes to this problem. Obviously, don't carry a Smart Device or turn it off when You don't wish to receive calls. Other solutions include placing calls from another smart Device and leaving your Smart Device off. Thus, responses to that third phone do not disturb you. Another solution is to leave a voicemail response to calls which direct the caller to send you an email. Leave an email address for response. Another approach is to use Facebook or Twitter to communicate and receive return messages.
>
> Unsolicited messages are non productive uses of your Smart Device message allowances. Most carriers provide blocking methods. However, they vary slightly from carrier to carrier. The blocking methods also include helpful tools. You may reach these blocking methods at these addresses:

AT&T: mymessages.wireless.att.com

Verizon: text.vzn.com

Sprint: sprintpcs.com

T-Mobile: my.t-mobile.com

Yahoo Mail: mail.yahoo.com

Sales calls may be blocked by getting listed on the national "do not call" register@donotcall.gov. That web page also has a complaint form. (ref: PC World).

A Checklist for Defective Smart Devices:

Your new smart Device will not turn on. Make sure you have installed the battery correctly. Check the manual.

The smart Device turns on but does not make calls. Check the SIM card. Is there one installed? Is it the Correct SIM card for this geographic area? Is it inserted correctly. Check the manual.

The smart Device is working but reception is poor, loaded with static or you are dropping calls. Check with you carrier.

The customer service phone numbers for the United States are:

AT&T Customer Service: 1-866-246-4852

Nextel/Sprint Customer Service: 1-800-SPRINT1

T-Mobile Customer Service: 1-800-937-8997

Verizon Customer Service: 1-800-922-0204

How to improve smart Device signal reception

The solution is called a "Femtocell". This special box is available from smart Device providers. It receives and sends smart Device signals via personal smart Device tower via DSL r cable internet connection, and then broadcasts the signals with the user's smart Device. The units are carrier provided, including:

AT&T: The 3G Microcell, $ 149.99, provides data and voice up to 5,000 square feet.

Sprint Wireless: Airwave, $ 99.99 plus $4.99 per month: Provides signal for voice only up to 5,000 square feet.

Verizon Wireless: Network Extender, $ 99.99. Provides signal for voice only up to 5,000 square feet.

(Ref: WSJ).

Getting out of a Smart Device Agreement:

If you are not getting what you want out a smart Device agreement but are reluctant to pay the cancellation fee, consider a smart Device contract swapper. cellswapper. com is a web site where you can pass your smart Device contract to someone who wants it. For example, you have five months left on your smart Device contract. With Cells swapper you list your plan and reach someone who enjoys service from that carrier and would be happy to assume your contract for the remaining time. You are free to act and the other party has a good deal with no activation fee and a short term contract.

Chapter i-7

Smart Device User Interface

Purpose: Describe the Desirable Smart Device Interface

Action: Use the desirable attributes to guide application design.

Applications Are The Key To successful Smart Device Use.

Applications are the lifeblood of Smart Device Usage. Applications are pre designed software packages to speed your use of a Smart Device. They are intended to save you the effort to design and program a solution which you will need to successfully use your Smart Device. The Application is a solution that was designed and implemented by someone to save you that effort. In some cases they are provided free of cost by the Smart Device provider to support his product and make it more attractive to buy and use. In other cases, it is the product of an entrepreneur who observed a need and prepared the application program for sale. In either case, it is an attractive attribute for the Smart Device you want to acquire and use.

The Smart Device display is the principle interface to the user. Its goal is to quickly communicate to the user the nature of the application and to enable quick user response for option selection, information entry and action initiation. As stated previously, the goal of effective user interaction is to achieve a "Learning Curve of One". The Smart Device display is probably the single most important element needed to achieve the "Learning Curve of One". This guide will try to provide guides to make more effective use of the display. They will highlight those display characteristics needed to aid in achieving that goal.

Basic Design features and Goals:

* Reduce the number of elements per screen
* Limit the number of colors used, font and size
* Use contrasting colors between the foreground and background, and providing lots of white space.

Content:

* Avoid overcrowding the display.
* Better to spilt content into two or more displays.
* Try for a consistent style across all applications.

Clarity:

* Simplify design, features and content.
* Keep logos and ads to a minimum.
* Home display to be bold, colorful and lots of contrast Avoid full screen videos.

Call to Action:

Be explicit.

Consequence of pushing a button must be clear !

Offer feedback on progress.

Search feature not reasonable.

Keep data/content local.

Reduce amount of entry as much as possible.

Keep keyboard simple with sound feedback.

Try to avoid card based data capture. Use Smart Device contained data.

Test your proposed plan

When your design is drafted, it should be tested with a non participating person. Ask a secretary to try several transactions after a simple education period. That exercise will quickly demonstrate the value of your proposed action plan. Repeat the design phase to simplify the proposed design.

Chapter i-8

Smart Device Based Bank Organization 2026

Purpose: Describe the expected 2026 Smart Device, Internet based bank organization

Action: Use for establishing a Smart Device development plan of action.

The Functions:

The primary, government-licensed, bank functional units (teller, loan and payments) will be the same in 2026. The primary changes of 2026 will be in the implementation of each function. The former implementation with paper based, manual processing and local handling will be replaced. It will be replaced by Smart Device based "electronic paper", electronic processing and remote Internet based processing. This will be achieved by the use of mobile transaction Devices, use of the world-wide Internet, and electronic logic implementation Devices.

What is the objective of this migration from paper and manual activities to electronic and remote Smart Devices? The changes have been for added productivity, speed, and convenience. You will be carrying a mobile Smart Device for many of your everyday activities. This will be another use of that Device. You will be using the Internet for many of your everyday activities. This will be another use of that network facility. Your bank will be keeping your account records, and handling your transaction processing and payments handling processing as part of their banking responsibilities. These are an added use of those Internet based facilities.

Teller Function Future

The 2010 Teller Function processes transactions. This includes receiving funds and cashing checks. This function will continue. Its implementation will change. Former branch activity will migrate to the automatic processing of transaction information through the Internet. The branch transaction activity will diminish to the point of disappearing. That means the face-to-face branch transaction use will decrease significantly.

Paper check handling will disappear. Two steps will need to be taken. The first step is to retrain branch transaction personnel to handle marketing processes in support of network activity. The second step is to prepare for branch conversion from transaction handling to customer support and education. This requires personnel trained to support digital banking Devices. Support personnel will need to understand the Internet, it applications programming, and transaction protocols. The bank will need application development resources that grow the use of the Internet. They need to continue simplifying the new mobile Smart Device and electronic implementation of the Internet based teller function.

The 2026 "Teller Function" challenges include:

> Getting customers to use Internet facilities.
> Accommodating different customer experience segments.
> Keeping up with financial needs of Internet based shopping.
> Innovating fast enough to meet use Improving our process.
> Site performance monitoring
> Relate to our web site performance
> Dealing with user privacy concerns

Loan Function Future

The Loan Function receives and lends money. This takes many forms ranging from overdrafts on checks to long term home mortgages. This vital function will continue with use of the Internet and electronic applications. Lending applications will be available in electronic form.

This process is dependent on users accessing the correct process and procedure for the desired loan. Trained bank staff will be available to assist the loan process online or at local support centers. Approved loan proceeds will be made available through the Internet based Teller function.

The Loan Function has the same challenges listed above for the Teller Function. In addition, the Loan functions have these added challenges:

> Validating remotely located resource value.
> Accommodating different community valuations.
> Including exchange variations, when applicable.
> Producing locally acceptable documentation.

Payment Function Future

The Payment Function implements the flow of funds between banks and their customers. It has the same challenges listed above for Teller and Loan Functions.

Transitional Demands

The migration of teller transactions from in-branch face-to-face human transactions to remote self service, Smart Device based Internet transactions will have a number of added impacts. Branch, personnel, rules and audits will all face the need to reshape themselves for a paperless, card-less, and all electronic new environment.

Facilities will need to be remade for the new approach.

Personnel will need to be retrained. Support systems will need to reflect the new implementation requirements. The challenges listed above are the basis for the new preparations required. To replace face-to-face transactions will require "Personal Profiles". This is a collection of customer based facts to substitute for a teller's personal observations. These include the customer's language, eyesight, financial package experience, and the like.

The future branch will need to be guided by these goals:

1. Build Smaller, but maintain location visibility.
2. Design smarter. Do away with teller stations. Develop a greeter and sit down station.
3. Use technology. Offer video conferencing with bank specialists.
4. Use wall mounted displays with touch technology.
5. Cross train staff to provide all needed functions.
6. Improve staff retention for these higher power staff members.

Bank Industry Standards

Standards are industry based agreements to uniformly organize shared or interchanged information, processes, or Devices used in the industry. Digital banking in the year 2026 will be preceded by standards for bank industry based Internet use, related Devices, communication protocols, and the replacement of former paper based documents and their processing. These standards will include electronic money, mobile Device based transaction cards, URL based account access, Personal Profile data, and other Internet based mediand their processing. The international (ISO), national (ANSI) and industry (e.g. ABA) standards groups will need an early set of specific standards objectives to achieve an orderly and timely transition to Internet based Smart Device based implementation.

II Smart Devices and Banking

Chapter ii-1

The Changing Role of Banks

Purpose: Projecting the bank to Smart Device evolutionary changes.

Action: Assign resources for an orderly migration.

2010 to 2026—A decade of branch bank to Smart Device role change:

The forces for migration of the bank to a Smart Device based role change will include: (1) the rapid growth of smart Devices and smart phones as the prime vehicle of individual communications, and their replacing transaction cards; (2) the role of the Internet as the dominant world wide communications network in almost all industries including bank, health, retail, education and government; (3) the disappearance of paper in the bank industry, including the growth of e-Money (electronic money), check images, and remote/interactive self service; and (4) the migration of bank to Smart Device systems from stand alone facilities to Cloud systems with the removal of all geographic and physical boundaries.

Migration of the Bank to Smart Device Relationship Role

Branch banks continually undergoes change. These are changes in bank ownership, processes, equipment, computer applications, marketing and customer interface. These changes occur over an extended period.

Changes leading to the branch of the 2026's actually started in the 1980's. The sequence of changes, as summarized by industry consultants, was as follows:

1980/89: Growth of Automatic Teller Machine (ATM) and Call Centers started to "invite" transactions to leave the teller based branch. The branch role was reduced to 85% of their pre 1980's manual teller, 90% of their manual teller branch role.

1990/99: Automatic call centers, ATM saturation and the growth of check and cash alternative deposits reduced the branch role to 65% of their manual teller branch role. The branch sales role was reduced to 85% of their manual teller branch role.

2000/09: Online Smart Devices became routine **including online account opening. The decline of paper checks is aided by check image processing and smart Device capture of check images. This reduces the branch role to 35% of their manual teller branch role. The branch sales role is reduced to 75% of their manual teller branch role.**

2010/19: With a completely electronic bank to Smart Device system conversion, the branch role is reduced to service customers who are 50 plus years old. This reduces the branch role to 15% of their manual teller branch role. The branch sales role is reduced to 50% of their manual teller branch role.

2026/29: New customers were raised on a smart Device environment with full Internet use. This reduces the branch to a small niche serving older customers and some urban concentration areas. This reduces the branch role to 10% of their manual teller branch role. The branch sales role is reduced to 20% of their manual teller branch role.

These branch transaction mode changes are summarized as follows:

Year	s 1980/89	1990/99	2000/9	2010/19	2026/29

Transactions (As % of pre 1980 teller branch activity):

Teller	90	75	35	15	5
ATM	5	10	15	10	5
Phone	5	15	25	20	10
Online	–	–	25	55	80

Service (Process requests)

Teller	85	65	35	20	10
Phone	15	35	45	30	15
Online	–	–	20	50	75

Sales (Account acquisition)

Branch	95	85	75	50	20
Phone	5	15	15	5	5
Online	–	–	10	45	75

Branch Impact:

Branch relevance is eroding. The new technologies of Smart Devices offer self service banking. Consider the Chase example:

Smart Device Applications—Chase is a Good Example:

See (chase.com/mobile web page)

Required for access:

> Mobile Device with Android Operating System
> Chase Online User ID Password

Applications:

> Pay bills and Credit Card accounts
> Transfer between Chase accounts
> Send wire transfers to non Chase accounts
> Find Chase branches and ATM's
> See account balances and transaction history
> See Credit Card and Debit Card Awards
> Receive and send text messages at no charge

Interfaces to all major mobile providers

Other Banks offering Similar Smart Device Applications:

> Bankofamerica.com
> Suntrust.com
> Ally.com
> USbank.com
> Wellsfargo.com: Personal loans
> RBCRoyal.com
> Citibank.com/citimobile

Smart Device Migration Joins the General Economy

World wide e-commerce migration is the basis of branch changes. These changes come from the emergence of new tools and techniques being used by the general public. Many of the new Smart Device customers of the 2026/29 era will be weaned on smart Devices in the previous decade. Many of the older Smart Device customers migrated to smart Devices and Internet usage in the previous decade. Hence, branch bank to Smart Device conversion is only reflecting the migration of the general population to the new electronic communications products and their functions.

Smart Devices Need to Prepare for the New Internet Functions

Actually, even with the changes projected here for Smart Devices, the branch changes are lagging behind the changes taking place in other industries. Retail sales on the Internet really lead the way into this new e-commerce era with its new communications and payment options. Using Google "Shopping" on the Internet to do a product search for a retail offering allows the buyer to visit and compare the offerings of hundreds or thousands of sources in a fraction of a second. The Smart Device industry will be a similar target with the migration to the Internet. Hence, branch bank to Smart Device evolution needs to prepare for the e-commerce era.

The army of earlier tellers will likely be replaced by smaller teams of trained Smart Device customer interface service representatives. They will be available in non-branch population centers. They will combine aggressive marketing of Smart Device based banking and its services with usage guidance and demonstrations of new products and services. The service representatives will work with electronic displays in other environments such as sports and entertainment venues. In other words, the bank's Smart Device marketing challenge will be to find or make community hubs where service representatives can interact with the public and potential customers.

New Smart Device Functions will Emerge

The Smart Device based electronic bank of 2026 will require a control center. It will be designed to access account and customer data on a real time (immediate) basis. It will have access to customer account history. Also, it will have a "Personal Profile" of the customer including: language spoken, eye sight level, prior account experience and prior financial education or demonstrations. This profile will be used by service representatives as a basis for action. The Personal Profile will also be the basis of programmed actions. Application programs will use the Profile to personalize its actions when responding to customer requests and actions.

A comprehensive description of Smart Device products including services and rates will be available. Predictive models will be available to make risk assessments for actions to be authorized. Secure access will give control center personnel account access to monitor and respond to remote customer requests.

Security Functions

Biometrics will play a significant role in Smart Device based banking security systems. Routine fingerprint scanners will be used with remote electronic acceptors. That will avoid password entry and keyboard use. These will be augmented with voice recognition or image/facial based identification. In addition, Smart Devices will be equipped with Near Field Communications (NFC) contactless identification for non contact acceptors. These will work at up to 10 centimeters or 4 inches distance from wireless phone to acceptor. That close distance will severely hinder attempts at eaves dropping on the NFC transactions.

Branch, Services and Technology Migration will Reduce Costs

Two important economic changes will occur by 2026. The cost of the electronic Devices will fall. The wireless Smart Device cost of 2010 will be reduced by up to 80% by 2026. This was the same experience with the early magnetic striped cards whose prices dropped from $2.50 each to $0.25 each during their first decade of use. Then they fell to $ 0.025 in the next decade. The price reduction came from technology improvement and economies of scale.

An equally important cost reduction will come from the vast increase in self service with an almost 90% reduction in branch face-to-face, teller based transaction requirements. Magnetic cards will be replaced by longer life electronic Devices. The electronic system will provide better security and loss controls. Removing paper from the Smart Device system will eliminate check handling, statements and postage costs. The totally online system will provide better loss and fraud protection. Both facilities will eliminate all of the manual activities associated with check and card based systems. The customer will provide the Smart Device infrastructure.

Migration Paths Needed to Achieve the Smart Device Bank

Critical to the migration from the paper and manual bank to the Smart Device based electronic and self service bank will be the disposition of the paper based products and services. The products and their dispositions are:

> Money: Paper, coins and transaction cards (magnetic Stripe and Smart (EMV) cards), to electronic value, accessible with a mobile Device such as a Smart Device.

> Checks: Paper to check images, to captured images such as a Smart Device based camera/optical capture of a check image, and to an electronic message on the internet.

> Contracts: Paper to electronic documents with encryption protection and electronic access keys.

> Counter services (e.g. deposits and withdrawals): Paper transactions replaced by direct electronic transactions. They are protected by encryption and electronic access keys. The transactions are implemented with a self service facility, using a customer supplied Smart Device to establish identity, and to provide secure controls.

> Marketing Smart Device services introduction: Interactions with branch tellers are replaced by remotely located service personnel or electronic messages associated with other electronic transactions. Use of the Internet also allows replacing static page images with continuous action video presentations. Marketing will also use prepaid smart Devices as introductory Devices.

Mobile Devices Enable Product Implementation

The evolution of smart Devices into computers that allow telephone calls, called Smart Devices, will provide a wide variety of Smart Device product functions. These will include computer applications (pre programmed solutions) for these functions:

Currency conversion calculations
Loan calculators
Mortgage calculators
Language conversion
Smart Device product menus
Smart Device department lists and access addresses

Tax calculations
Physical parameters conversions

Introducing the Digital Wallet for the PayWave Service

The Visa Digital Wallet uses Near Field Communications (NFC) with Visa's PayWave service. The goal of the new service is to transform the way consumers pay for low value items. (From Mobilepaymentstoday. com/article_print/181276). The PayWave technology is contactless and is designed to make a transaction in less than a second without the use of a PIN. The transactions are made using NFC communications. By 2010, Visa PayWave was used in Europe with pilots underway in most European countries. Public transport journey payments are expected to be a major future use of this technology. It is quick, convenient and does not need a separate ticket or travel card.

Smart Device Management Actions are Required

The evolutionary changes described here are well underway. It is imperative that senior bank management recognize that the changes are underway. Their setting new management goals and objectives will allow the changes to best achieve their image of the future Smart Device facilities. In all cases, fine tuning to the customer set, physical and municipal environment, tax and regulatory demands, and available financial status are necessary ingredients in achieving evolutionary success. Face to face transactions will be replaced by Smart Device applications. The Smart Device Bank facilities of the 2026's will demand the best of bank management supervision and skills.

Chapter ii-2

Smart Devices, The New Bank Systems Tool

Purpose: To further elaborate the Smart Device role and functions.

Action: Require assigned organization responsibility to elaborate on their planned use of these functions.

Introduction

Just as the magnetic striped card marked the start of the self service banking era forty years ago, the Smart Device marks the start of the "Mobile and Internet Based Banking Era". This era will be marked by paperless banking, Internet communications with wireless based mobile interface Devices and customer supplied infrastructure. The critical building block will be the customer and employee carried Smart Device. The Smart Device combines self service with direct, communications based, data base access. That combination offers speed of action with simplicity of operation. Self service is the direct benefit of forty years of magnetic stripe based self service.

What are the System Attributes of a Smart Device ?

The Smart Device is a hand-held, mobile communication Device, that receives and transmits voice, data, audio and video based information. It communicates with short-range transmitters strategically located in small geographic areas or "cells". The transmitters recognize when the mobile Device physically moves. The system logic automatically "hands" the communications interface of the Smart Device to the next small area transmitter as the mobile Device changes its geographic location. The communications operation is fully duplex. It transmits and receives on two different frequencies.

The Types of Mobile Devices

The basic Device is generally referred to as a Smart Device. It is a hand held, mobile, wireless based telephone. It has the basic functions required by a communications Device:

> Dialing keyboard
> Battery power supply
> Speaking Device or microphone Hearing Device or ear phone.
> Display of called number
> Display of calling number
> Manufacturer's identification
> Assigned serial and phone numbers
> A microchip insertion card
> Provides carrier connection information
> Internal circuitry for sending/receiving communications
> Internal logic for any added functions
> Indicators for signal strength, power level

In addition to the Smart Device there are Devices for recharging the contained battery. These allow charging in conventional power plugs and in mobile vehicles. There are a variety of radio connection capabilities. Some operate with remote antennas. Others operate with close-by radio frequency based connections.

Smart Phones

These are hand held computers that also act as mobile Devices. The Smart Device adds a number of communications based, computer-like applications and functions, well beyond those of the mobile Device. Included are:

Computer functions

Operating system
    Controls hardware and software
Browser (Web access) software
    Download and send email
Wide variety of user selected application programs
    e.g. mortgage calculations
    e.g. currency conversion
    e.g. anti-virus software
Keyboard
Function keys
Synchronize data with external computer
Work with attached documents

Multi-media functions

Transaction cards stripe content capture
    Selective transmission
    NFC wireless connection chip (two way)
    Two way allows password entry
Camera—picture and video
    Check image capture and transmission
Image viewer and streaming video
Audio capture and playback
    Play recorded music
Touch screen controls
Record/image filing and recovery
Image identification capture
Geographic Positioning System (GPS)
Color controls and support options
Instant messaging send and receive
Digital memory cards interface
Printed optic code scanning and conversion

    Converts to a URL for Web access.

Smart Device Use Reports Your Position and Actions

Considering privacy requires that the Smart Device users understand that they are leaving a trail of information. Every time the Smart Device is turned on, it reports its position to the national mobile Device system. That is the means by which the Smart Device system knows where to find you when you are to receive a call. Furthermore, communications with others such as a retailer, leaves a trail of information on the goods purchased, where they are delivered and the method and account for payment.

Related Devices are Converging

E-Readers provide an electronic display of book based documents. A low cost version of the laptop computer, the Netbook, also provide for data display and can simulate the E-Reader. Both Devices offer an ability to display contract related information and other documents. Thus, they have a potential role in the all electronic bank. Simulating the E-Book offers the added ability to use the other functions of the lap top computer to communicate, to access data, to interface the Internet and to carry and execute application programs.

The Smart Device Era Bank Branch

The migration of branch face-to-face transactions to the Smart Device on a self service basis will have a significant impact on branch size and function. The branch function will shift to marketing, new customer indoctrination in Smart Device based banking and supporting the transition. The design will incorporate table displays. Here the marketing representative and the Smart Device oriented customer will meet over a display table. The table will project a visual display of the bank product being offered. It will allow interaction for key variables such as length of loan, interest rates, and amounts. The branch might not shrink too much in size but the use of space will be much different.

The future branch will be a greater user of technology. Interactive display stations will communication with bank specialists in other geographic locations. Prerecorded sessions will help to educate customers about product offerings. Self service tablets will facilitate customers in form filling and product applications. Interactive displays will give immediate access to historic records and current market conditions to speed transaction decisions. Also, the future bank branch will need a personal profile for the customer. This will be a substitute for the lack of face-to face transactions and the teller's personal insights. For example, what language does he speak? What is his eye sight to automatically adjust display characters size? What is his past experience with assorted bank products ?

New Personnel Training

The branch personnel will need more extensive bank function and bank product education. The former teller will need to acquire marketing and financial advisor skills. These added skills will be required to keep up with a growth of interactions required by the capabilities of their expanding technology tools. Consider the skills needed to introduce the customer to Smart Device banking. With some ten major brands of Smart Devices, their operation, their applications and their bank's own banking applications, that will produce a large number of combinations. In addition, for each bank Smart Device application there will be a number of product and service attributes that the bank personal will need to understand, explain and interpret.

A byproduct of the growing branch personnel sophistication will be the need for a concierge at the front door. That function will be needed to meet and greet the customers. Most important will be their skill needed to understand the customer's requirements, to direct them to the correct branch personnel, and most important, to know what the customer needs to do to prepare for the branch personnel availability. These skill needs will be multiplied by the need to understand the products offered by bank suppliers such as the card networks (up to five, and growing). That will also bring along issues such as why doesn't my Smart Device work properly, or where can I get it fixed.

The New Competition

Retailers are offering financial products for less than the cost of ikeit competitors as it does for dry goods, dairies and food products. They don't produce the financial products. They offer the products of other financial institutes. The products are offered in low-cost facilities which share the high traffic of the retail establishment. The traffic is low end demographics that use their lower end facilities and services. The retailers do not face the same regulations as bankers, which further reduce their costs and prices. The retailers also offer banking in the same aisles as their dry goods shopping.

New Technologies offer New Facilities

Welcome to the wonderful world of technology and their application expansion. Consider the new concepts of an electronic wallet and Near Field Communications (NFC). Each are major new capabilities but they need explaining and usage assistance. These new facilities will also require application downloading stations. The new facilities will also create a new set of questions about charges, billings and their payments. The wallets introduce SIM cards for their use, and the network attachment they provide. In addition to their national usage, the next customer through the door wants to go overseas and needs guidance on how to get Smart Device usage in a half dozen countries. With a 40 to 50% annual transaction growth, the Smart Device will be used for mobile purchases and payments.

How big is the new Smart Device banking market ?

These issues will give you a grasp of the subjects which will be discussed in further Chapters. The 7 billion world inhabitants are already using more than 5 billion mobile Devices for more than 2 billion accounts and as a growing substitute for 6 billion bank cards for over 12 trillion dollars of transactions with a 68% annual growth in Smart Device based transaction for payments

Chapter ii-3

Card and Check Migration to Smart Devices

Purpose: Understand the key banking transition issues to Smart Devices

Action: Establish a plan, with incentives, to make the switch.

Introduction

The magnetic striped card, its successors and MICR (magnetic ink character recognition) based checks are fundamental financial instruments for the 2010 bank. The objective of the Smart Device Bank 2026 is to eliminate all paper and paper related instruments. That does not mean eliminating the function provided by those instruments. Rather, it means applying a modified process which allows most bank customers to accept and use an alternative paperless process which produces the same usage results as previously produced by processing paper and cards.

Check Migration

Check migration from paper to electronic image began before 2010 with the advent of check image processing. The written check was image captured at the first point of bank acceptance. That could be high speed check processors or check image capture in Automatic Teller Machines. Physical check return disappeared with the printing of check images for return to the writer as part of the monthly statement. Or, for display with online bank check statements.

Physical check entry to the bank disappeared with the advent of check image capture in ATM's, smart Devices and Smart Devices. However, the real test is the process by which the individual originates a check based payment. The payment needs to identify the payer and the payee. Where bills are being paid, the payee is identified by the demand for payment. The optical image feature of the Smart Device can be used to capture that data just as it is used to capture check images for processing.

Where the payer is originating the payment, the payee is identified in several ways. One is by a keyboard entry in the Smart Device. The second is by maintaining a list of payees and indicating the one chosen for the payment. A third way is by using a numeric code for payees and extracting the appropriate entry from the bill to be paid. The numeric index extracts the full payee designation from a previously established data base. When all other solutions fail, the payment can be made to cash. Then, accompanied by a letter of instruction identifying the payee.

The Check Replacement Goal

The real goal of all these processes is to eliminate paper checks, and to replace them with an electronic message. Once society recognizes the move to eliminate checks it will find other techniques to construct electronic solutions for payment processing. The key unit of mobile banking, the Smart Device, will become the payment vehicle of choice. Technology will continue to contribute to a mobile Device with advanced functionality. It will have all the attributes of a stored program unit, with preprogrammed applications, data bases and full communications capabilities. The mobile unit will have the capacity to initiate several types of payments. These include personal payments, business payments, family or trust payments and other categories. A number of alternatives to check payments is growing at an astonishing rate. These include PayPal, PaySimple, CashEdge, MoPay and Square to name a few. The result is that check volumes are decreasing by 10% per year or 7 billion few checks written annually. In fact, eighteen countries have announced the end of their check systems. The UK has set 2018 as their target to end their check system.

The Yankee Group forecasts for the value of US digital banking transactions as:

Year	Value
2011	$ 210 Billion
2012	400
2013	600
2014	800
2015	1100 (Wall Street Journal, 6/29/11
2016	1400

The Plastic Transaction Card Replacement

The financial transaction card offers two data streams. One is the visible data printed on the card. There are also characters embossed with raised, but readable fonts. The second data stream is recorded magnetically on the magnetic stripe. The latter requires a magnetic reading head and associated circuitry. Later cards, such as Smart (EMV) cards provide data through electronic contacts on the card surface. The data comes from a micro circuit chip embedded in the plastic transaction card.

The magnetic stripe data for the bank industry consists of 40 numeric digits, of 5 bits per digit, with a one bit redundancy. There is a second track of 79 characters, of 7 bits per character with a one bit redundancy. The latter track content is used by the travel industry since it includes the card holder's name. With a digital bankingunit it is easy to accommodate several track recordings, representing several different plastic card equivalents.

The Plastic Card Equivalent Transaction

Use of the digital banking Device as a magnetic striped card equivalent signal source requires a wireless transmission from the banking Device to the signal accepting unit. A NFC, (near field communications) signal is emitted by the digital banking Device. The digital banking Device displays the striped card equivalent type designation. A record is captured in the digital bankingunit for later reference, if needed. The acceptance Device processes the "card" transaction into the banking system. The variable amount of the transaction is added to the signal transmitted in the NFC signal to the accepting Device. The complete transaction data is then processed by the banking system.

The bank system processes the "card" transaction in the normal manner. The "card" is checked for being current and valid. The value amount is checked against the available transaction balance. Security checks are implemented against the "card" data, and any personal identification codes, if used. The transaction data is captured for account records, merchant records, and bank based controls.

A new data item is the mobile Device identification. A new check is required against the identification of the digital banking Device. Is it reported lost or stolen? Is it a legitimate transaction Device? Is this the authorized user of the mobile transaction Device? Is the application program being used authorized and the latest available version? In other words, the switch to a digital banking Device transaction requires that it be legitimized, as were transaction cards.

Introducing Mobile Device to Mobile Device Transactions

The NFC Near Field Communications function is a two-way function. That allows, with appropriate application programming for the digital banking Device, transactions which transfer value from mobile Device to mobile Device. With the mobile Device carrying monetary value, it increases its use and applications. Eventually, with wider availability of NFC function at point of sale, cash registers and Automatic Teller Machines the expanded mobile Device function will eliminate the use of paper currency and coinage. That will eliminate the concern about counterfeit cash. However, the concern will then shift to the mobile Device and its security. There are adequate protection techniques, but they need to be implemented.

The Transition to the Paperless Bank

The real issue is the ability of bank customers to shift to the new digital banking instrument, the Smart Device. The 40 years of magnetic stripe usage in self service units has set the stage. The decades of smart Device usage further confirms the ability of the bank customer to adapt. The world wide acceptance and use of Smart Devices clearly demonstrates the ability of all economic and education strata of society to adapt. The growth of lap top computer use was another predecessor of the digital bankingunit.

A further aid will be the use of the Personal Profile for each bank customer. The bank system will know the experience level of each customer. That will allow the bank system to adjust to the bank customer's experience. Using the digital banking Device display, the bank can issue appropriate directions to the customer to assure a correct response to the checkless and cardless type transactions.

Chapter ii-4

New Smart Device Banking Role
and Revenues in 2026

Purpose: Describe the new Smart Device revenue opportunities in 2026.

Action: Assign application development responsibilities for 2026

Doing Bank Business in 2026

The changes projected for the bank of 2026 will eliminate the conventional needs for a bank branch office. However, the 2010 branch was the prime location for face to face banking transactions. The teller was expected to sell accounts upagerading with added bank products and services.

A Four-Step Process—Step One

Preparing to do banking business in 2026 will start with a four step process. Step one is to physically identify the new customer. This includes capturing a physical identification and the related biometric characteristics. It also includes capturing identifying numbers such as a social security identification and/or a federal tax identification number. Step one also includes the start of a "personal profile". This includes eye sight characteristics, language spoken, education level, bank product experience and hand writing characteristics. Those characteristics are used to automatically adjust the interactive, programmable logic to the customer's bank product experience and to adjust the display characteristics to the bank customer's needs given by the customer's personal profile. Thus, enabling the 2026 bank systems to match the needs of the bank customer, without the benefit of a teller and a face-to-face transaction.

The Four Step Process—Step Two

Step 2 of doing bank customer business in the year 2026 is to identify the financial needs of the customer from a banking point of view. What type of accounts does the customer want or need ? What has been the customer's experience with your financial products? Those characteristics allow the bank system to interact with the bank client at a level which optimizes to the client's understanding. It allows the bank systems to provide training and know how to support the marketing of new banking products and tools.

The Four Step Process—Step Three

Step 3 of doing bank business in the year 2026 is to establish the client's financial objectives. What are your resources? What do you need to accomplish financially? What portions are savings? What portions are for investment? What portions are for transactions? These objectives enable the banking application programs to monitor your financial activities. More importantly, your financial objectives allow the application programs to measure your actions against your objectives.

The Four Step Process—Step Four

Step 4 of doing business in 2026 is to instruct the bank system about your preferences for the digital banking Device or Smart Device you will use. This dialog will continue for as long as you use the same mobile Device. There are a large number of application programs available for most digital banking Devices. As the Device user updates the mobile Device application programs, the banking system will need to stay up to date on the user's preferences and usage status. The mobile Device, the Smart Device, will need to be kept up to date with account numbers, security solution in use, and funds availability.

The Smart Device and Tablet Banking Services

A recent Yankee Group Report concluded that the consumer interest in digital banking results from these factors:

The services were largely free.

The 25 to 34 year old age group were most responsive.

The users tended to be more affluent

That managing account balance was the top activity.

Second was funds transfers

Third was locating facilities, e.g. ATM's and Branches.

Initial use was high but after a few months leveled off at 12 to 14 activities per month.

Users saved money by avoiding fees associated with late payments.

Younger clients (under 25) are more security conscious and try to save money by transferring between accounts rather than use ATMs and pay their fees.

Use of NFC was the largest fee opportunity because it offered micropayments and ease of paying transit fees.

Digital bankingoffers these services:

Checking balances

Paying bills

Transferring funds between accounts

Finding nearby branches and ATMs

Offering 24/7 services

Visualizing account status and cash flow with rich displays and charts.

Accessing personal money management tools and tips.

Check balances and recent activities

See available balances and credit lines

View minimum payments and due dates

Read up on personal finance and money management

A very useful aspect of digital bankingwere sending messages and enrolling in educational opportunities. In other words, expanding the use of mobile Devices to better understand and use the new services and facilities.

The Bank Revenue Sources in 2026

The bank customer of 2026 has access to a broad array of communications and data base facilities. Many of these offer important economic advantages to the bank customer. As a direct consequence these facilities also offer the providing bank with new revenue facilities and opportunities. The bank customer will have a growing stable of electronic Devices. In addition to the mobile Smart Device banking Device, there is the e-Book, the compact laptop, and the Geographic Position System (GPS). These Devices are part of a growing collection of programmable Devices with compact or virtual keyboards and displays, attached to the Internet.

These bank facilities offer important data base access. For example, there is access to stock market data and planning models. There is access to immense data bases including individual directories, search data bases, and geographic data bases. The mobile Smart Device Devices offer camera functions, still and motion. The camera offers Universal Product Code capture and automatic conversion to URL based Web page addresses. With a preprinted menu of Web pages, the Smart Device banking unit can be used to provide direct access to a full menu of bank products and services.

In other words, the Smart Device based banking Devices of 2026 will provide the bank customer with access to programs and data bases which can produce new revenues for the bank customer. In turn, the bank can charge for use of data bases, access to them, use of models and even a percentage of the new revenues they produce.

The New Smart Device accessible

Network Facilities Offer New Results

The Internet will be the key communications facility of the 2026 bank.

The Internet is a world wide facility. It offers, in addition to data access, both audio and video capabilities. This opens other functions to the remote banking unit. These include world wide Smart Device based communications, access to video programs and educational materials. Inquiries by bank customers into bank products for which the customers have no previous experience will immediately result in presentation of an educational package. The package will educate the bank customer in the product capabilities, how to use it, and will offer an assessment of early customer produced experiences to improve their usage.

The Green Revolution, A New Banking Opportunity

An important ecological trend is the Green revolution. It offers a number of planning opportunities to reduce power consumption, or use the power available, with a more economical and energy savings mode. These are the popular options:

> Solar power
> Heating and cooling
> Lighting
> Irrigation

These and similar proposals share the same needs. They need access to planning and financial models. They are natural users of the expanded communications facility of the 2026 bank. As the mathematical models assist in design and implementation, the user will need access to financial loans. The 2026 bank will offer a number of educational and planning models to assist and implement these efforts. Like wise, the future bank customer will respond to bank initiated marketing efforts offering similar results.

The New Roles and Results of the 2026 Smart Device Based Bank

Google offers a "Shopping" mode. It searches the Internet for a category of products selected by the user. For example, searching for "Energy Saving Products" produces over 100,000 Web page hits. That is an opportunity for the 2026 bank to combine user education with potential uses of financial loans. Similarly, a Google search on Solar Power produces almost 85,000 hits.

In other words, the 2026 Smart Device based banker will need to understand the Internet resources available with the new communications capability. Key is how to convert these search results into future bank product marketing opportunities. The 2026 banker will need to convert his selling activities from the 2010 branch office lobby to the 2026 Internet "lobby". Offering 2026 banking facility will be materially assisted by the Smart Device based communications capabilities of the 2026 bank system and tools. The conversion of paper instruments of the 2010 bank to the all-electronic bank of 2026 will materially assist the 2026 banker to offer significantly new bank assistance and new revenue opportunities.

Chapter ii-5

Bank Branch Economics 2026

Purpose: Describe the Smart Device based bank economics of 2026.

Action: Start a 2026 financial plan, with a focus on preparing to gather the 2026 specifics.

The 2026 Branch Function and Features Will Be Different:

Banking processes and practices in 2026 will be much different than 2016. The laptop will be gone the way of the desktop computer. Computing capabilities using Smart Devices will exceed those of the desk and laptop computers used in 2016. Tube and flat screen displays will be replaced by pen size projection Devices using flat surfaces such as walls. In other words, computing power will be mobile, portable and pocket size. They will give bank customers direct access to their own private computer power and personalized data base storage located in distant Cloud computers.

The paperless bank, tied to the Internet, will offer customers all branch functions of 2016 from their Smart Device banking unit. The "virtual" branch, functionally, as we knew them in 2016, will provide access to all banking functions, and to a small team of service oriented bank staff advisors. The advisors will have access to your Personal Profile and your personal data bases to answer your banking requests and questions. You will have access to training tools to help you understand and use the full array of Smart Device based bank products.

The branches as we knew them in 2010, with staffs, physical space and counters will be a remote memory. Branch functions of sales, tellers, and

ATM's will be replaced by the "virtual" and paperless branch accessible via your digital banking unit. Paper checks will have disappeared and were replaced by electronic equivalent capture, transmission, interchange and electronic access of check images. Paper and coin currency will have disappeared and were replaced by electronic money usable by NFC communication from your Smart Device banking Device. Electric money will be transferable from mobile Device to mobile Device, and to NFC interconnected communication Devices.

The New Bank Economics

The bank of 2026 will be considerably different with staff use and facilities. That will not necessarily reduce the cost of providing the bank. There will be major changes in the mechanization and supporting personnel. The physical branches size will decrease significantly. However, there will be expenses associated with smaller service facilities and remote Cloud facilities. There will be more expenses associated with maintaining the software and data bases need to support the new branch equivalent virtualization structure.

Moving to the all electronic bank will also move the bank to a 24 hour, seven days per week response organization. The bank structure will be much more unattended. However, that requires operating facilities, power on, with fully operable communications and network services. Money will go into facilities to support this type of operation, their operating and maintenance staffs.

The Major Economic Challenge

The basic requirement of the 2026 bank will be the digital bankinginterface unit, the smart Device or the Smart Device. This unit will be carried and used by the bank's customers and by the bank employees. These represent two types of funding issues. First, dealing with the bank's customers. Obviously, the most desirable solution will be that the customers provide their own Devices. That will require an immediate effort by the bank industry to prepare a set of standards that define the interface required between customer's digital banking Device and the bank provided Internet interface. That is identical to the concept of a standard magnetic stripe card of the previous forty years. The internationally standardized striped card was universally accepted as the customer carried Device to interface to ATM's, point-of-sale units, and teller units.

The majority of customer carried digital banking Devices have application interface ability. One of those applications will be the interface to the bank industry via the Internet. For the relatively low cost of creating the international standard, the customer's will provide their own digital bankingcapability in their own provided mobile Device.

The second issue is the digital banking Devices carried and used by bank employees. There are two approaches to these units. One is to have employee personal Devices which also have a bank interface, such as the standard interface provided by customers' own units. These might be funded by an allowance paid to the employee. The second are bank provided units. These will need a provision for employees to pay for personal use of the units. To keep this process as simple as possible, it is recommended that a standard allowance be offered to avoid complicated bookkeeping requirements.

These two solutions are offered to keep the economics of a large quantity of digital banking units within a reasonable range.

Smart Device Economics

Most Smart Devices have the same total cost over a 2 year contract. Consider these three examples:

	BlackBerry	Apple	Palm
Cost of the Smart Device:	$ 200	$ 200	$ 300
Less mail in rebate:	(70)	–	(100)
Activation fee:	35	38	36
Total (+ Sales Tax) Monthly Charges:	$ 165	$ 236	$ 236
Unlimited talk (Domestic):	100	100	100
Unlimited text"	20	20	Incld

Unlimited data:	30	30	Incld
Monthly Total:	150	150	100
Total 2 year contract:	$ 3765	3836	2636
Monthly cost:	$ 157	$ 160	$ 110

If you are seeking lower costs, consider low cost mobile Device such as the Palm. An even greater gain can be achieved by going to a prepaid T Mobile service for smart Device only. That would lose Internet accessed applications—but would give a lower cost alternative.

A New Approach

The new facilities, described for the bank branch 2026, will be the default platform for the competitive bank of 2026. It will take good banking skills to provide the new bank products and Devices that will make the new bank happen, and be usable by the full range of bank customers. Competition will be the driving force for this new environment. A key concern is that the Internet is an international Device. That will allow a banking institution ANYWHERE IN THE WORLD to be your competition. The large scale systems capabilities of China and India will be on your front door with an Internet facility.

The Internet is a world wide competitive Device. Computing Clouds from Tata in India and the equivalent organizations in China have another big asset. Their countries have the largest economic resources due to the national loan position of the United States. That fact, coupled with their labor know how and education will combine to create an even more capable competitive force. Banking is a universal skill, a universal need and a universal response. The issue is no longer the cost of the new approach. The issue is how to survive and thrive in the improved and world wide Internet based digital banking technology environment of 2026. The major branch productivity improvement with Smart Devices replacing face-to-face transactions will need to be balanced against the growth of competition. The best defense still appears to be an aggressive employment of the Smart Device and its important application attributes. Now is the time to prepare for this bank industry change.

Chapter ii-6

Security Architecture for Smart
Devices Based Banking

Purpose: To provide a checklist of security issues to be faced for Smart Device based banking systems.

Action: Requires an early start on a 2026 security architecture.

A Recent Survey

"Only one in five consumers feel protected from fraud during mobile banking." From a recent study by ThreatMetrix and The Ponemon Institute. In other words: Digital banking has a long way to go to gain consumer confidence.

Introduction:

The Internet is a collection of networks. They carry a variety of services—text, audio and video. The Internet has no central management or authority. Hence, security must be an individual using organization responsibility. There is no facility to protect the data traffic. Security tools do exist. Some of the security tools are off the shelf. Other security tools are created by the using organization.

As an Internet user, you must understand your own requirements. As a user, you must provide key information such as credit card numbers. The merchant provides important information in the form of receipts and payment information. Vital data flows in both directions. Hence, your security objectives must describe your possible exposures and your planned responses. A security approach must be selected, implemented and the response evaluated for adequacy. Any solution will involve trade offs. The user must decide where to draw the line between expense and security adequacy.

A security architecture is required. It must match the security needs with the chosen solution. It measures security solution performance and adjusts the results, as needed. Start with a risk assessment. Require the participation of all major organizational functions.

The Risks

Unauthorized information access and its misuse: There is a great deal of valuable information in these systems. Credit card numbers, passwords, balances, access codes, digital certificates, and so forth. There are a large number of individuals with access including account holders, family members, bank employees, and communications employees. In addition there are attackers seeking to get access to the valuable information in order to attack the system. There are a variety of attack scenarios including eves dropping, wire tapping, capturing radio waves and misusing various system elements.

Service interruption or degradation: There are a number of deliberate techniques to interfere with normal system operation. There are a number of accidental ways to interfere with normal actions. Hackers spend hours testing their ability to penetrate these operating systems or to interfere in their normal actions. Attacking supporting systems such as power and air conditioning also produce abnormal system actions.

Privacy violation; Disclosure of information which the owner considered his own. Disclosure may be intentional by others or accidental by the owner. In either case, the damage has been done when the private data becomes publicly available. The damage may not be evident to others.

Vandalism, sabotage, and viruses: Attempts at forging an email address, or overloading a system with an over abundance of email destined to one address or using fictitious addresses to disrupt normal system operations or generating false requests for vital data re all forms of attacks in this category.

Errors or omissions: These attacks may be accidental or deliberate. Application specific controls may be violated. In either case, dropping key data will result in abnormal operation.

Unauthorized systems usage: Release of vital information by searching or unintentional disclosure may lead insiders to exercises which bypass normal controls. Also, maintenance activities may produce results which are unanticipated but dangerous. A more sophisticated attack may attempt to take control of the system without normal supervision. Disgruntle employee actions may also contribute to this type of attack.

Unauthorized software usage or copying: This type of attack is particularly possible from employees without proper supervision. They also may be stimulated by outside software provider employees. Another source of this attack is the use of commercially available software without reasonable controls to prevent copying or unsupervised usage. Also, software must be considered as a source of attack.

Spyware can hijack your smart Device. It gives an external hijacker complete access to all of your actions including hearing conversation near the phone. It can turn on your unit remotely. Spyware is illegal but is available in other countries and through the Internet. There are a number of techniques for accessing your phone, including selling it installed with the unit. How do you detect spyware ? Your phone bill shows unknown phone numbers. The battery is warm when the phone is not in use, or dies quickly. The phone flickers when not in use. Prevention includes locking the phone when not in use and don't open email from unknown sources. The best defense is to buy a low cost, prepaid phone for sensitive conversations.

Mobile Threats: Lost and stolen Devices; Malicious software (Malware); Unauthorized network access using lost and stolen Devices; Unauthorized access to data with lost and stolen units; and unexpected disasters.

Fraudulent Application Programs: For example, a value transfer application is being distributed which identifies itself as coming from a legitimate bank. The program actually transfers value to a fraudulent recipient.

Innovative PIN Code Attacks: A recent innovation in PIN attacks is to access the PIN pad shortly after the PIN code was entered. The keys are photographed with an infrared camera and shows the "finger heat" on the keys. This reduces the unknown digits, even after five minutes, to four of the 10 keys. With 12 combinations of four "heated" keys as a possible PIN code, it reduces the unknown combination significantly. Hence, use of a PIN code is compromised by this technique. This produces a significant PIN code weakness. (See hackedgadgets. com/2016).

The Lines of defense

Encryption: as a security process requires the use of controlling keys, similar to a combination lock's opening value. Not all data needs to be encrypted. Certain vital data, such as a PIN value, or an access code needs to be protected. There are a variety of encryption techniques which vary by complexity, effort needed to decode them and number and length of keys required. Systems management needs to select the correct characteristics. Tamper proof containers need to be used to protect keys between usage. Keys need to be protected (encrypted), if broadcasted in system usage.

Digital certificates: application of encryption process to a specific file, database, transaction or other collection of information. Used to detect any change in the content. Valuable in authenticating messages, assuring the equivalent of a signed document, and detecting any unauthorized tampering with transmitted data, payments, or software.

Key management systems: handling of encryption keys including their generation, transmission, protection and automation of the entire process of using encryption keys. An effective system assures frequency of key changing and their usage protection. It will also detect weak keys and their misuse.

Time and date stamps: Electronic equivalent of postmark which assures the time and location of data authentication. Used to support other controls such as key management. They are used for definitive proof of an event's occurrence.

Password authentication systems: Fixed passwords authenticate a user's identification. However, they are considered as weak. They can be intercepted, recorded and replayed. Products are available that encrypt the passwords and make them look different each time they are applied. Attackers will create dummy log-in screens to capture fixed passwords. A useful defense is to require two or three factor identification such as a password and a magnetic stripe recording. A finger scan might be added for three factor identification.

Dynamic password systems: The password is changed each time it is used. There are a variety of techniques on which to base the change. It may require a fixed password to initiate operation. This may also require a synchronizing process to get various system elements to operate properly with each other.

Biometric authorization systems: Based on a measurement of a part of the user's body such as voiceprints, fingerprints or signatures. This check may require a "learning" process to teach the sensor receiver about the users' characteristics. These are becoming available as built in to Smart Devices.

Privileged access control systems: Access may be limited to certain days or hours of the day or other pre specified windows of operation.

Firewalls: A pre specified test of incoming data to establish its acceptance for entry. There are a variety of techniques based on the type of information being filtered. Sometimes the rejected data may also be killed or terminated. In some cases, the users may add their own tests after the firewall. Virus detectors may also be added. Periodic testing of the firewalls are needed to check that their operations have not been changed by an attack.

Logging and real time alarms: These are added to other defenses to measure the number and source of security hits. These include automatic notifications, messages and audio alarms. The recorded logs need to be protected to prevent the hiding of attacks. One approach is to place the logging Device in a locked container.

Automated auditing systems: The operations staff runs auditing software systems. There is also software in firewalls to alert the systems administrators. Some is run as often as daily. They generate reports showing excessive user accesses and identify system vulnerabilities. They also identify unusual credit card usage patterns. Other software identifies database handling issues and computer game playing.

Network management: Software monitors network operation for unauthorized activities and unusual transmission error rates. This software monitors problems remotely and can fix some problems. The software integrates security alarms into the network management system.

Virus protection systems: These detect malicious software and unauthorized codes. The primary source of viruses is the Internet. Hence firewalls should provide virus scanning and rejection capabilities together with backup system software. Scanning should examine files going in both directions so that yo are not the source of virus infections. Activity logs should be kept to detect the virus sources. A continuous update service should be used to identify all the potential viruses. Some viruses will disguise themselves. Hence, a second screening by a different anti-virus software is necessary.

Software management systems: These systems prevent running unapproved or unlicensed software by using encryption processes. Special software can search to assure that the software used is properly licensed and is the latest version.

Data and message filters: This software records the web sites visited and the time spent at each. It blocks improper URL use. This requires using a service which lists current prohibited addresses. The filters also prevents downloading unauthorized software. Passwords control software downloading. Filters are also sensitive to information classifications and will not pass secret information without a suitable password.

Backup and recovery systems; A recovery plan must be specified to follow a serious problem. Software packages are available to help construct recovery plans. To be effective, periodic backup steps must be taken to assure that the correct backup materials are available. Clean power sources must be available to support the backup effort.

Payment Clearing Services: Organizations involved in payments processing require a legally enabled back up facility to clear payments following a systems failure. The backup process must produce a legal receipt for the transferred value. The entire process must be reviewed by the regulatory authorities, before the fact, to assure smooth recovery.

Mobile Device Security: Physical locking cables; User authentication with passwords and biometrics; and data protection with encryption and the ability to remotely erase lost an stolen unit content.

Mobile Network Security: Device authentication; Virtual private networks with secure access; Firewalls to filter unwanted attacks; Systems management for program patches and upagerades; and Policy Enforcement with clear and timely communications.

"Cards Not Present" is a key security condition on a card network in dealing with mobile Devices: Responding to these transactions requires a comprehensive fraud screen. That requires: Intelligence about usage patterns; Online and off line purchasing profiles, Identity of risky transactions, comprehensive and frequently updated views of usage, and a willingness to decline risky transactions.

The SPARC (pat pend) Smart Device Security Solution:

The SPARC Device works with any Smart Device using any communications protocol. Applications issued by a Financial Institute (FI) are programmed to require the preparation of a message to the FI to be preceded by a message to the SPARC Device with the account identification. The SPARC Device must be within 10 cm of the Smart Device.

The user agrees with the message by actuating the SPARC push button. There is NO requirement for PIN entry. The SPARC captures the account number and issues a one-time identification code. The code is returned to the Smart Device, where the ID is inserted into the message to the FI and the message is sent to the FI. The FI evaluates the one-time ID when compared to an image of the SPARC's data content kept in the FI's data base. When approved, the application is performed and the result is returned to the Smart Device with another one-time code. If the Smart Device is lost or stolen, its controlled applications are not usable without the companion SPARC unit. The SPARC unit may be used with several applications from the same FI. (Contact the Smart Card Institute for further details(smart Device @ sprynet.com)).

Phone Factor

When you log into your bank account, PhoneFactor initiates a process which calls you at a pre established phone number. You answer the phone call and enter your PIN code to complete account access.

Advantages: Protects you even if someone has your PIN number. Protects against a lost and stolen Smart Device on preprotected applications.

Disadvantage: Needs an available phone number, and preferably a mobile number. Needs to key in the PIN number. Protects at start of transaction. Does it protect the application response? Does not protect against line taping message and recording PIN for later replay. Does it protect PIN value in communications?

Smart Device Security Solutions

There are a number of Smart Device security applications available. For example, Smart Device security programs offers the following components:

> Secure the Smart Device with a strong password protection
> which the users can not turn off.

Use an application which can remotely lock the Smart Device if it is lost or stolen.

Use an application which allows wiping data from the Smart Device memory remotely, when required.

Encrypt sensitive data stored in the Smart Device.

Distribute and install security program patches as required and administrator controlled.

Automatically back up vital data from Smart Devices Under administrator control.

Distribute and install antivirus and software patches immediately and under central control.

When a Smart Device connects to the system check who is accessing data and applications. Block any unprotected Devices by authenticating users and Devices.

Block any network intrusion by unauthorized access or unprotected Devices. Centralize control of security policies with audit security automatically enforced.

Security Architecture Summary:

This menu of security checks offers a starting point in constructing your security plan. The Smart Device based banking environment of 2026, with its need for new corrective actions, will be an invitation for attackers to be inventive, and they will be. It is essential that bank resources start now to prepare its 2026 security architecture.

(FOR DETAILED SECURITY MATERIAL SEE XLIBRIS BOOK "SECURE YOUR INTERNET USE").

Chapter ii-7

Smart Device Based Mobile Banking

Purpose: Introduce portable Device initiated banking.

Action: Assign resources for an orderly implementation.

Items Required For Mobile Internet Access

The challenge for those desiring access to all the resources reachable by the Internet is to provide a basic set of functions. First requirement is the mobile Device—a smart Device, a Smart Device or a PDA (Personal Digital Assistant). All have display and a keyboard. In addition, they have a communication interface and the logical capabilities to talk via the network. Second requirement is to have a software package called a Browser. The browser has the software interface to satisfy the protocol or information requirements of the network. The third requirement is a data plan which allows the mobile Device to carry on transactions between the mobile Device and the application providers reached by use of the networks.

There are a variety of applications accessible by the Internet. They provide these mobile accessible services:

Information: Applications are designed to add information to the accessible data. Also, to use the accessed data to achieve desired results for the access Devices and Smart Devices.

M-Commerce: The unit participates in commercial transactions with value exchange.

Email and Instant Messaging: Information is provided to achieve the information exchanges and commerce required interactions to successfully complete transactions without regard to geographic location or time of day induced limitations.

User generated mobile Web sites: There are a complete set of tools, technologies and services available to all the participants to make your claims by the mobile accessible network.

Mobile Internet for Business: All types and sizes of businesses have the Internet resources available for their use in their business activities.

Mobile applications (software): Application programs needed to produce results through use of the Mobile Internet are available for all participants.

Information for entertainment purposes: Applications range from pictures, to games, to music and lectures. All provide audio/visual stimulation and logical stimulus.

Use of Mobile Devices

Use of mobile Devices provide experiences which are much different than dealing with the Internet alone. The mobile Device is a very personal unit. It accompanies the user through a broad set of communications and experiences. The process of communications reaching you with the mobile unit requires a specific phone number which accurately identifies the recipient. Built into the mobile Device process is payment. The mobile Device offers several payment alternatives, as arranged by the user. All of these mobile Device capabilities, provide the user with a functionally valuable Device.

Smart Device Based Digital banking Related Definitions

Digital bankingis the use of a portable communications Device to access and use financial services. This concept is well established with the use of wireless phones to find bank account balances and their status. As portable communications Devices evolved into Smart Devices, portable computers that allow phone calls, their banking functions further increased in sophistication. For example, Smart Devices are now being used to capture and transmit check images for electronic deposits. The portable Device also runs banking applications. For example, they can be used to calculate currency conversions or mortgage loan tables.

Digital banking also includes the use of portable communications Devices to make payments. These applications result in the portable Device replacing the use of financial transaction cards. Using contactless functions, the Smart Device will have a short range (to 4 inches or 10 centimeters) NFC Near Field Communications capabilities to the transaction acceptor. With the representation of monetary value by an electronic record, the portable Device replaces one or more magnetic striped or smart financial transaction cards and replaces Automatic Teller Machines. The electronic information will be secure with the use of encryption or other protection schemes.

The Factors for Going Mobile

The reasons organizations introduced digital banking services in the United States are:

87% Added service to improve customer experience.

81% Competitive advantage

71% Logical extension to Digital banking

65% Customer demand

55% Reduce existing customer service costs

48% Reaction to competitive mobile services

39% Generate new revenue streams

Growth factors

The expansion of digital banking results from several factors. The magnetic striped financial transaction cards have been used in most industries and by 80% of the world's population. The card accepting Devices, such as Automatic Teller Machines and access Devices have taught most of the world's population to use self service operation. The use of striped tickets in mass transit have also taught the public to accept and use another form of "self-service". The designers of the card accepting units have been careful to design simplicity into their operation. Thus, self service was further established as a normal mode of operation. An added consideration is the cost of and maintenance expense of Devices such as the Automatic teller Machine. Also, the cost of loading currency and removing deposits from those Devices. Those expenses disappear with the move to Smart Device based monetary transactions.

The Wireless Phone

The wireless phone has also evolved over time. It has always been a hand held Device. The initial use was as a telephone with key driven operation. Even as the smart Device evolved into a Smart Device based portable computer with sophisticated display and computational facility, it remained hand held and operated. The main enhancement has been the growth of "applications". These are preprogrammed computer solutions to a variety of practical needs. At least one of the current crop of portable computers has more than 450,000 such preprogrammed applications available for use. Even as smart Device unit suppliers have tried to inhibit other suppliers of functions, we hear of "unlocked" and "jail broken" attributes. Both of these terms mean that the unit has been opened to function and applications beyond the constraints of the original unit manufacturer and communications carrier.

Thus, the combination of self service, portable computational facility and application programs, have created the "mobile banking" facility. Ease of use, variety of applications and sophisticated problem solutions have created the modern digital banking facility. In addition, the solutions have had security processes built into the units and their application operations. These offer banking, payments and funds transfer results. Thus, use of the wireless phones have resulted in the bypassing of former banking solutions including branches, ATM's and their paper based instruments.

Contactless and Wireless Functions

Contactless function allows card based functions without inserting the card into a card accepting Device. The interaction is achieved through the used of electromagnetic ("radio") signals radiated from the transmitting Device, e.g. the contactless card. There are several types of signals. However, the dominant type appears to be the Near Field Communications (NFC) standard which requires that the transmitter and receiver be within 10 centimeters or 4 inches of each other. This greatly inhibits use of a listening Device to steal the information being transmitted. The transmission may be two way or bidirectional. That allows applications which add information, such as current account balances, to the portable Device.

Wireless function replaces electrical line usage with radiated signals. For example, even an ATM might be installed without the use of a connecting telephone line. This avoids the restrictions and expensive of a physical line(s). It can provide both voice and signal connections. It eases the deployment to remote sites. It may require a power line. However, even the power line may be replaced by a solar power facility with battery support for power storage in dark periods. Those wireless functions reduce installation and communications expense. They speed the installation. However, they may require adding security Devices, such as a GPS (Geographic Positioning System) unit, to insure that the unit is physically located correctly, or has not been moved without permission.

Mobile Self-Service Options

Use of mobile Devices allows twenty four hour operation, seven days a week (24/7). Also, operation comes close to providing "no-wait" customer service. There is little restriction on the information available. The available information includes:

Accounts balances
Accounts statements
Recent transactions history
Check and transaction status
Funds transfer and bill payment status
Deposits and withdrawal management
Access to loan accounts and transactions

Payments and due dates
Access to account and usage blocking
Customer requests status and replies
Access to cash dispensing at merchants
Portable Device to portable Device communications
Loyalty incentives and status
Pension plan management
Tax records and status
Language translations
Facilities locations for banks, merchants and postal
Ordering account options and media
PIN and security management
General information such as weather forecasts

A very important functional capability of mobile operation is the availability of immediate alerts. These are immediate advices to the portable banking Device user of banking conditions requiring their attention and action. These include:

Credit/debit limit and status alerts.
Minimum balances
Bill payment reminders
Interest and exchange rates changes
Overdraft alerts
Fraud alerts
Stock quotes
Requests for voice communications
Security alerts and changes
Stop pay actions and status
Emergency and "911" requests.

Alternative to a Branch Closing

As the digital banking Devices and their acceptance become more wide spread, there will be transitional issues. Perhaps the most serious is the issue of "standards". That is, the need for a consistent interface between all of the participants. These include merchants, other banks, government agencies, other individuals and other mobile Devices. These start with the basic data representation, radiated signals, message formats, and transaction types.

Add to these the international travel requirements and currency conversion needs. Most of these needs are the responsibility of industry associations' activities and International Standards Organizations.

Consistency of Portable Device Actions and Operations

Fundamental to any society is the availability of many suppliers of equipment and systems. These too will need to present a consistent method of operation and user communications. The financial institutions' associations will need to publish their communications and presentation needs. These will be used by the portable Device manufacturers to prepare to interface to their planned solutions. Just as coin and currency conventions were used in the paper based environment, similar information will be fundamental to the sound operation of the new digital bankingsystems. In a similar manner, security plans and responses will need to be understood by the suppliers and users of the digital bankingequipment and systems.

Personalization of the mobile Device operation is an important consideration. The unit will be used with a variety of companies and in an assortment of physical locations. Key personalization factors will require:

Owner/operator identification
Preferred organizations identification
Special needs such as application experience
Touch screen preferences
Preferred language

Date/time zone and format
Default transaction preferences
Beneficiary identification
Preferred time responses
Mobile Device screen, functions and applications Interface
needs e.g. Visa, MasterCard, Amex, etc.

Summary

The all electronic, Smart Device based bank of 2026 was preceded by forty years of self service experience starting with the magnetic striped bank card and the Automatic Teller Machine. Advent of other card technologies continued to confirm the bank customer's willingness to use self service.

The mobile smart Device and Smart Devices continued the trend but added the non contact attributes to the process.

Forty years of progress in reducing the size and increasing the functionality of electronic Devices have brought the banking industry to the enviable position of combining functionality with portability. The sharp reduction in dependence of the industry on paper instruments has been an added benefit. The next forty years should be more exciting.

Digital banking Internet References:

www.casisoft.com www.clairmail.com
www.clickatell.com/solutions/financial.php
www.firethornmobile.com   www.fidelityinfoservices.com/
fnfis
www.fiserv.com www.frondeanywhere.com www.gemalto.
com/financial
www-03.com   /industries/financialservices/us/index/html
www.jackhenry.com www.m-com.us www.mfoundry.com
www.mmventures.net www.pyxismobile.com www.s1.com,
www.postillion.com www.sprint.com/finance www.sybase.
com/365 www.tyfone.com www.verisign.com www.yodlee.
com

III Smart Devices Applications

Chapter iii-1

Smart Device Based Mobile Banking Applications

Purpose: Describe the Internet based Smart Device transaction process in sufficient detail to produce application specifications.

Action: Assign process and program function steps to the Internet application development function with appropriate completion target dates.

Introduction:

Many of the concepts and processes that will be described for Smart Device based, Internet based, banking are also applicable to other industries. Retail, health care, and others industry applications will use these same type of techniques and processes. It is like the magnetic striped credit card. It was originally designed for use with banking and airlines. They are now use with every industry, world wide. More on these other industry electronic Internet usage opportunities later.

The Digital banking Business:

Migration to a Smart Device based, all electronic banking concept will have significant impact on conventional banking facilities. It will impact the physical attributes of the branch. Tellers for transaction processing will disappear as they are replaced by remote self service. It will significantly impact the roll of branch banking personnel. It will significantly reduce physical efforts such as mail delivery and processing. It will replace physical money and check security needs with network/ electronic based security functions and strategies. Visits to the "branch" will be accomplished electronically. The business of electronic banking will be 24/7. Successful bankers will need to move rapidly to keep up with the rapidly changing, remote, electronic functional, Smart Device environment.

An all electronic, Smart Device based banking environment offers significant improvements in delivering bank products. It will offer faster delivery to most remote transaction locations. It will exercise better controls. Perhaps, more importantly, it will quickly identify new options and opportunities for using bank services and products. As the number of Internet based bank products increase, it will be essential for the banking systems to follow the customer's use of bank processes and to then make suggestions. The suggestions will be based on a customer's personal profile. More on the "Personal Banking Profile" (patent pending) concept later.

Surviving as an Internet Banker:

One last observation before the details. You will read about many new concepts associated with the Internet based, Smart Device based, banking environment. Understanding and applying them is not an option. The most desirable set of bank customers—the young and electronic game trained crowd—have the ability to rapidly acquire your new products and services. In other words, your survival as a banker in this new banking era will depend on your ability to understand, accept and stay ahead of these concepts at a rate equal to that of your youngest and most aggressive market place customers.

The Electronic Bank:

The all electronic bank of year 2026 will use the Internet to provide bank account records, access and all "branch" type functions and transactions for customers using the Internet. Smart Device based access to the 2026 bank, with all electronic accounts, will start with the URL (Internet address) of the Web page assigned to the customer's account. An explicit URL will be a unique Web page address for each customer's bank account. The customer's Web page, in turn, will provide direct access to all bank relations for that customer.

(Note: The application solutions that follow are similar to the solutions required in other industries. Bankers should look at this similarity as an invitation to provide services to organizations in other industries such as Retail and Health/ Medical. There is a range of services the bank can offer. They range from guidance in development to providing the full solution to an organization in the other industry. In either event there is a revenue opportunity to the bank wishing to assist other industries to use the new Smart Device based, paperless, internet based transaction processing solution).

The Conventional Bank Account Relations

The conventional bank branch provides a wide variety of bank products and services, with supporting personnel, equipment and with well established paper instruments movement:

Types of funds: Cash, checks, cards, etc.

Funds usage: Deposit, withdraw, transactions

Loans: application, withdrawal, payment

Instruments: purchase, cash-in

Investments: types, purchase, cash-in

Product knowledge and questions

Branch personnel

Branch equipment and facilities

Night depository; Safe deposit, ATM's

Security systems, alarms, and network attachment.

Physical facilities, teller cages, work rooms

The Conventional Branch Method of Operation

Account relationships generally started with a meeting with a banker. The meeting was used to educate the potential customer. The types of services and accounts available, their operating requirements, balance requirements, and the identification required for use are described. In addition, arrangements need to be made to issue check books, access cards and access keys, if needed. Initial deposits are required to fund accounts. Identification pictures are taken, when required.

Transition to Smart Device based Electronic Banking

It is important to recount the requirements for conversion from a conventional account to a Smart Device based electronic account. All of the paper based, manual functions and Devices need a replacement in an all Smart Device based electronic banking system. Consider these changes from the paper bank to the all electronic Smart Device based bank:

From: (Paper)	To: Smart Device based (Electronic)
Paper checks	Check Image
Credit cards	Smart Device wireless
Paper currency	Electronic Message
Paper contracts	Electronic Document e-Book Display
Coins	Electronic Message
Physical keys	Electronic Message
Physical signature	Digital certificate
Fingerprints on paper	Biometric identification Voice print

Goals of Mobile Banking: The real value of Digital bankingincludes:

(1) Providing access to account balances.

(2) Transferring balances between accounts in the same bank.

(3) Sending funds to accounts in different Financial Institutions.

(4) Opportunity to pay bills.

(5) Sending funds to others.

In other words, Digital banking gives customers more control of their finances. It also significantly reduces staff based inquiries and transactions. The net result of offering Digital banking is:

(1) Provide customers with complete account access and use.

(2) Offers secure transactions with the available functions.

(3) The Smart Device service is reliable.

(4) The self-service transactions are cost effective, with a customer provided infrastructure.

(5) The process is adoptable to further account Development and offerings.

The Customer's Web Page

The customer's assigned web page is his "permanent" interface to the electronic bank. It is accessible from anywhere on the Internet. It requires that the user has a "Browser" type software program that interfaces to the Internet. The browser takes the customer's URL from a key entry or any readable medium, such as a magnetic striped transaction card. The Browser then interacts with the Internet control process to reach and retrieve the addressed personal Web page.

Consider a bank provided personal Web page with the following information:

> Name and contact information for Web page holder
> Name of the banking institution
>> Password process to open for use Contact information including:
> Web Page designation,
> Mailing address, email address,
>> Federal clearing number,
> Bank relations including association,
> Credit card processors, and telephone numbers.
> URL of Personal Profile (age, sex, eye sight, hearing, language, education, account experience, and bank history).
> Federal, state and local tax status and numbers.
> Related facilities such as a vault.
>> Protected (hidden) access codes, pass words, biometric characteristics, and security preferences.
> Transaction value limitations if pre specified.

Each current account by type and access number:

> Balances
> Transaction record
> Funds status and availability
> Accrued interest
> Current charges
> Action limitations, if any.
> Related account actions required.

> Added Web pages are accessible to hold data. For example, transaction records would be kept on related Web pages which are easily accessed for inquiry.

Transactions in the Smart Device Based All Electronic Bank of 2026

The customer is provided with a mobile transaction Device. Typically this is a Smart Device with Near Field Communications (NFC) wireless connection to a NFC accepting Device. The Smart Device may contain the equivalent of the magnetic stripe content for several different bank, transaction and access cards. The stripe content for one bank card contains the URL for the card holder's account accessible through the Internet.

The URL is used by the browser program to access the web page of the card holder. The first step after reaching the web page is a request for a user password entry to establish the correct user of the access program in the mobile Smart Device. An incorrect password entry stops the process and returns the process to password reentry. After a specified number of password entry failures, the web page access is denied.

With the opened Web page, the user selects the bank service desired. For example, the user wants to reload value in the mobile Device. The user is asked to specify the amount of value requested. The requested value is transmitted from the bank system to the mobile Device for later use. Suitable records are transferred to the bank systems for periodic statements and appropriate bank records of value dispensed. All actions are examined by appropriate bank control and security programs.

The user is asked if there are any other transactions required. If not, the session is ended with a suitable display of the account status at the end of the transaction, such as remaining account value.

Summary

The all electronic, Smart Device based bank of 2026 was preceded by forty years of self service experience starting with the magnetic striped bank card and the Automatic Teller Machine. Advent of other card technologies continued to confirm the bank customer's willingness to use self service. The mobile smart Device and Smart Devices continued the trend but added the non contact attributes to the process.

Forty years of progress in reducing the size and increasing the functionality of electronic Devices have brought the banking industry to the enviable position of combining functionality with portability. The sharp reduction in dependence of the industry on paper instruments has been an added benefit. The next forty years should be more exciting.

Chapter iii-2

Internet Role In Smart Device Banking

Purpose: An introduction to the Internet.

Action: Establish your bank's focus on the Internet.

A Note of Caution:

The Internet components—applications, services, Devices, technologies, vendors, users, protocols and standards—grow and change each year. This description focuses on the elements critical for your successful Smart Device use of the Internet. However, this material needs to be updated when used. Key Web page addresses, (Domain names or Uniform Resource Locators, URLs), are included to help you quickly assess the latest Internet status. A key information source is the Internet Retailer Guide to E-Commerce Technology (internetretailer.com).

The Internet allows access from more points, more quickly and more easily than any other network in the history of networks. Thus, along with its new facilities comes new and serious security exposures. Since there is no central authority dealing with these security exposures, you, the user must insure that you are protecting your Internet plans and programs. This Chapter will describe your Internet facilities. The Chapter on security will describe the options for your action to protect your Internet plans and programs. Please take this note of caution very seriously. There are security tools to protect your Internet actions. Your goal must be to use them effectively.

Initially

The Internet was an electronically connected set of computers with a common information structure, format and information encoding. It was intended to share available computer time between government supported computer installations. The objective was to use their surplus available computer time to solve large computational problems associates with atomic energy development. It was also intended to provide an ability to share facilities in case part of the facilities were destroyed. The communications structure was enlarged to include access to libraries and development records maintained in each of the participating organizations.

Eventually—Today

The Internet is interconnected public networks that are self supporting and run on a cooperative basis. All share a common data format and content code. That is a protocol called TCP/IP (transmission control protocol/ Internet protocol). The international association of companies that manage the Internet is called the World Wide Web (www).

Web Pages

The Internet provides Web pages. A Web page is a collection of text, graphics, sound and, sometimes, video. Together, they create a single window of scrollable materials. Hypertext is the text used on a Web page that leads the user to other related information, or Web pages. The Web page is found by a Browser. That is the software application program used to find and access a Web page.

URL or Domain Name

The Web page address on the Internet is called URL, a Uniform Resource Locator. The URL is the designation used by the Browser to access a Web page. Where does the URL come from? It may be found in the output of a Search function. It might be provided by the Web page provider to guide others directly to a Web page of direct interest such as a bank, retailer or health services provider. It may be found in publications, press reports, or directories.

As with any "address" it will be found with most communications vehicles.

Domain is another designation for the address of a Web site. It may be more than an address. If well selected, it may also be descriptive of the organization it addresses. The Domain name consists of several parts. The letters www. at the beginning of the domain name indicates the following information is an address on the World Wide Web. The last two or three letters of the Domain name indicate the Category of the organization named. It may be com. commercial, or gov. government, or org. organization, or one of several others. The latter designation may be followed by a designation of the country location of the originator, such as .us for United States, .au for Australia and .jp for Japan.

Email

The most widely used internet application is email. That is a message with a stated Internet destination and from an Internet source. It is also a vital marketing tool. It drives business results in the form of increased traffic, customer awareness and customer involvement. A recent Internet Retailer study showed more than 40% of business leaders were planning to increase their email marketing budgets. It will expand with a double digit expansion rate for the next five years. Why? Email is inexpensive. Email is effective because customers rely on it and marketing gets better results from its use. It is a frequent carrier of related URL's.

Favorite Function

An important function of the Browser is the "Favorite Function" (FF). It is a record of specific Web pages for recall later to provide quick Browser reentry to a Web page previously designated with the Favorite Function. It is a quick recall of a specific Web page, without going through a Web page search and discovery process. That discovery process would require a search operation and a search sequence output stream examination.

Use of the Favorite Function enables applications in all industries to go directly to a Web page of interest.

Use of the Favorite Function for a Banking Application

An Internet based bank provides each customer with a URL which uniquely identifies the location of the customer's bank data on the Internet. Using the URL in a Browser takes the user to an entry point for banking activities. The entry Web page will immediately impose further security control on access to the designated Web page. The software may ask for a Personal Identification number (PIN), a password established earlier, or a more exotic biometric Device output such as a fingerprint reader.

Successfully providing the entry control information, the program now allows a spectrum of banking functions. These range from simple inquiries to sophisticated loan requests and control reviews. There may be subsequent control features that respond to larger transaction values, value transfer transactions and sound banking criteria.

Specialized Networks

There are hundreds of specialized uses of the Internet. These are a subset of Internet use designed to interact with selected groups of individuals, corporations, religious, country residents, government agencies and the like. Their function is to allow the specialized participants to meet, exchange information and socially interact. Popular "Social Networks" include Twitter, Facebook, MySpace and LinkEdit. These networks offer low cost communications (plus the cost of the needed access equipment and software). In some instances, these networks reach up to two-thirds of a group's participants. Care must be taken to avoid or protect sensitive information. Participants need to establish and maintain lists of participants they want to reach in each type of network. From a marketing point-of-view these are excellent vehicles for programs designed to attract new clients.

The Internet is Essential for Smart Device Banking

The Internet is the vital element that ties all of the Smart Device banking units together into a working system. It allows the Smart Device unit to reach all of the data elements and software elements that combine to provide the banking services to the Smart Device user. Smart Device Bank 2026 provides significant productivity improvements to the banking industry. Your knowledge of the Internet and its role in Smart Device banking are essential for you to successfully build these working systems, and to realize their important results.

Chapter iii-3

Smart Device Accessed Internet Bank, Accounts and Transactions

Purpose: Describe the Internet URL based Smart Device transaction process in sufficient detail to produce application specifications.

Action: Assign process and program function steps to the Internet application development function with appropriate completion target dates.

Introduction:

The all electronic bank of year 2026 will use the Internet to provide bank account records, access and all "branch" type functions and transactions for customers using the Internet. Smart Device based access to the 2026 bank, with all electronic accounts, will start with the URL (Internet address) of the Web page assigned to the customer's account. An explicit URL will be a unique Web page address for each customer's bank account. The customer's Web page, in turn, will provide direct access to all bank relations for that customer.

(Note: The application solutions that follow are similar to the solutions required in other industries. Bankers should look at this similarity as an invitation to provide services to organizations in other industries such as Retail and Health/Medical. There is a range of services the bank can offer.

They range from guidance in development to providing the full solution to an organization in the other industry. In either event there is a revenue opportunity to the bank wishing to assist other industries to use the new Smart Device based, paperless, internet based transaction processing solution).

The Conventional Bank Account Relations

The conventional bank branch provides a wide variety of bank products and services, with supporting personnel, equipment and with well established paper instruments movement:

> Types of funds: Cash, checks, cards, etc.
> Funds usage: Deposit, withdraw, transactions
> Loans: application, withdrawal, payment
> Instruments: purchase, cash-in
> Investments: types, purchase, cash-in
> Product knowledge and questions
> Branch personnel
> Branch equipment and facilities
> Night depository; Safe deposit, ATM's
> Security systems, alarms, and network attachment.
> Physical facilities, teller cages, work rooms

The Conventional Branch Method of Operation

Account relationships generally started with a meeting with a banker. The meeting was used to educate the potential customer. The types of services and accounts available, their operating requirements, balance requirements, and the identification required for use are described. In addition, arrangements need to be made to issue check books, access cards and access keys, if needed.

Initial deposits are required to fund accounts.

Identification pictures are taken, when required.

Transition to Smart Device based Electronic Banking

It is important to recount the requirements for conversion from a conventional account to a Smart Device based electronic account. All of the paper based, manual functions and Devices need a replacement in an all Smart Device based electronic banking system. Consider these changes from the paper bank to the all electronic Smart Device based bank:

From: (Paper)	To: Smart Device based (Electronic)
Paper checks	Check Image
Credit cards	Smart Device wireless
Paper currency	Electronic Message
Paper contracts	Electronic Document
	e-Book Display
Coins	Electronic Message
Physical keys	Electronic Message
Physical signature	Digital certificate
Fingerprints on paper	Biometric identification
	Voice print

The Customer's Web Page

The customer's assigned web page is his "permanent" interface to the electronic bank. It is accessible from anywhere on the Internet. It requires that the user has a "Browser" type software program that interfaces to the Internet. The browser takes the customer's URL from a key entry or any readable medium, such as a magnetic striped transaction card. The Browser then interacts with the Internet control process to reach and retrieve the addressed personal Web page.

Consider a bank provided personal Web page with the following information:

Name and contact information for Web page holder

Name of the banking institution
Password process to open for use

Contact information including Web Page designation, mailing address, email address, federal clearing number, bank relations including association, credit card processors, and telephone numbers. URL of Personal Profile (age, sex, eye sight, hearing, language, education, account experience, and bank history). Federal, state and local tax status and numbers. Related facilities such as a vault. Protected (hidden) access codes, pass words, biometric characteristics, and security preferences. Transaction value limitations if pre specified.

Each current account by type and access number:

Balances
Transaction record
Funds status and availability
Accrued interest
Current charges
Action limitations, if any.   ,
Related account actions required.

Added Web pages are accessible to hold data.
For example, transaction records would be kept on related
Web pages which are easily accessed for inquiry.

Transactions in the Smart Device Based All Electronic Bank of 2026

The customer is provided with a mobile transaction Device. Typically this is a Smart Device with NFC Near Field Communications wireless connection to an NFC accepting Device. The Smart Device may contain the equivalent of the magnetic stripe content for several different bank, transaction and access cards. The stripe content for one bank card contains the URL for the card holder's account accessible through the Internet.

The URL is used by the browser program to access the web page of the card holder. The first step after reaching the web page is a request for a user password entry to establish the correct user of the access program in the mobile Smart Device Device. An incorrect password entry stops the process and returns the process to password reentry. After a specified number of password entry failures, the web page access is denide.

With the opened Web page, the user selects the bank service desired. For example, the user wants to reload value in the mobile Device. The user is asked to specify the amount of value requested. The requested value is transmitted from the bank system to the mobile Device for later use. Suitable records are transferred to the bank systems for periodic statements and appropriate bank records of value dispensed. All actions are examined by appropriate bank control and security programs.

The user is asked if there are any other transactions required. If not, the session is ended with a suitable display of the account status at the end of the transaction, such as remaining account value.

Summary

The all electronic, Smart Device based bank of 2026 was preceded by forty years of self service experience starting with the magnetic striped bank card and the Automatic Teller Machine. Advent of other card technologies continued to confirm the bank customer's willingness to use self service. The mobile smart Device and Smart Devices continued the trend but added the non contact attributes to the process. Forty years of progress in reducing the size and increasing the functionality of electronic Devices have brought the banking industry to the enviable position of combining functionality with portability. The sharp reduction in dependence of the industry on paper instruments has been an added benefit. The next forty years should be more exciting.

Chapter iii-4

Smart Device Applications

Purpose: Describe the Application Options Available

Action: Choose from Your Application Options

What is an Application (solution)?

An application is a software program designed to produce a specific result or solution to an identified need. It may also be a computer configuration (input, computation and/or result use) designed to achieve a specific result. An application solution may also be the use of Smart Device functions and features designed to achieve a specific result.

The objective of this Chapter is to provide the description of a number of application solutions. That will provide a basis for developing future application solutions. It should also provide a basis for managing the application development process. That includes estimating the resources necessary to achieve the targeted results.

The "application" concept has guided many companies in their organization and operation. IBM, during its formative years in the computer business, used "industry" as the basis for educating personnel and designing computer programs to achieve marketplace results. "Industry" was another word for "application" structure. It produced specific results for designated groups of customers operating in the marketplace. Similar goals were designated, and results developed to satisfy most segments of the economy.

Protecting Mobile Applications

A mobile application, like all written programs, is a literary work protected by the Copyright Act in the United States. You should consider registering your original work with the US Copyright Office. The name of your original app work should be registered with the US Patent and Trademark Office (The USPTO).

Marketing/Retail Applications

Recently released data provided these data:

> The National Retail Federation (USA) claimed that nine out of ten Americans have a Smart Device.

> Pew Research claims that 79% of English speaking adults use the Internet.

> Harris Research claims that the social lives of USA teens would end without their Smart Devices.

> Nielsen Surveys forecasts 120 million mobile Web users by mid-2016.

These data indicate that the general population has greater access to data than ever before. They also want to be connected to data regardless of their geographic location. Retailers have taken note of these marketplace changes. Mobile applications have been developed because they have the most potential to take advantage of these changing marketplace buyer characteristics. Consider these mobile changes:

> Mobile Ordering: Studies show that 20% of retailers have implemented mobile ordering applications. Quick service and Fast Food establishments are the leaders. They offer significant operational improvements and also lower labor costs.

> Mobile Inventory Control: These applications allow goods to be ordered from anywhere while being picked up it

specific locations. These applications have been attractive to Specialty Softgoods and Mass Merchandizing with more than 30% of buyers having made this type of purchase.

Mobile Price Comparison: This application has been least accepted by retailers, for the obvious reason that it encourages competition. It also encourages a customer to try to make a price deal. Hence, these application are in great adoption by customers. These are also available as a "Shopping" application in Google. They provide all Internet references to a given purchase objective. The application also provides sequencing by price (high to low, or low to high).

Mobile incentive coupons: The customer receives a coupon notification by email. The customer's Smart Device has a GPS function. It shows the nearest merchant location. At that location, a poster shows that the merchant is adding an additional part of the coupon offer. The customer taps his NFC Smart Device on the poster and the added offering is downloaded to his Smart Device. At checkout, the customer taps his Smart Device at the contactless (NFC) POS terminal to pay and to redeem two coupons. The net amount is deducted from the customer's Smart Device and the transaction is completed. Mobile marketing with NFC Smart Devices will enable consumers to signal their interest in various products and services by physically tapping their Smart Device on NFC-enabled product tags, shelf tags, smart posters, digital signage, POS equipment, kiosks, access controls, access controls and other objects. This very powerful functionality is interactive, real-time, personalized, and location-based. Retailers will be able to attract customers to their stores, gain brand loyalty and drive up selling opportunities. Secure chip technology enables multiple layers of security, including message authentication and data security for the coupons, payment information and personal information. The secure element may reside inside the Smart Device SIM, in an additional chip, or be added to the Smart Device in the form of a microSD card. Although this is a new application in the United States, successful Asia examples go back more than a decade. This application will unleash many more similar Smart Device applications in the future.

A number of Supermarkets use Smart Devices for self service activities. Stop and Shop in Massachusetts has a pilot program that enables customers to scan bar codes of each item they are buying and are bagging as they shop. The app is also linked to their customer rewards card so that they get targeted specials and coupons as they shop. This initiative reduces labor costs by 12% to 15% of the grocer's total expenses.

The Retail application for Smart Devices interface are designed to achieve these goals:

Inventory visibility: Availability regardless of location and addressable across different channels.

Order fulfillment: Automate an ordering process through a complex supply chain.

Order capture and management: Collect complete ordering information with full data capture flexibity and recovery.

Customer profile and history: Collect and used complete customer data and use it to create a complete shopping experience.

Pricing and promotions: provide complete and consistent prices and promotions regardless of customers' location.

Customer self service: Use customer's ability to implement all facets of the ordering and payment process after one experience.

Mobile Point of Service: This service uses a Smart Device in the hands of an employee to roam the store in peak periods and to check out customers before they get to cash register checkout points. It offers faster checkout to the customer. It relieves the cash register load. There are application programs available to facilitate this operation. The Aberdeen Group is preparing a detailed study outlining the options for this roaming Smart Device based service. Apriva, (Scottsdale, AZ, apriva.com) offers a Smart Device application that converts the unit into a mobile card processing terminal. Combining the software with an optional printer/magnetic stripe reader provides an alternative to a stand-alone credit card terminal.

A critical capability of Smart Devices is the ability to search price comparisons when retail shopping. Innovative applications are seeking out nearby customers and offering them incentives to relocate to their physical establishment. Check out shopkick.com. They offer incentives to relocate, physically.

In conclusion, the Smart Device is a valuable Retail tool. It offers these benefits:

> Pocket size power: It is basically a laptop computer in your pocket.

> Personalized information organizer: Provides access to diaries, contact lists and Internet assets.

> Direct information and communications access: Offers email access and other communication tools access.

> Accesses retail shopping information and searching tools, with faster communications.

US Army Readies Mobile Applications Store

The US Army is making a broad push into Mobility using Smart Devices and Pad Devices. They are working on 3 levels of security: Mobile Devices, Operating Systems and Authentication, and User ID.

They re considering biometrics such as fingerprint, face and voice recognition.

Smart Device Based Medical Applications:

Some of the most widely used mobile applications by physicians are drug and clinical references, and clinical tools such as dosage calculators. Transaction oriented, point-of-care applications, such as electronic prescribing and evidence-based decision support will be the next growing application category for the use of physicians' Smart Devices.

The number of physicians owning Smart Devices will increase to 81% by 2012. (See Global Mobile Health Market Report 2010-2015). These are a few examples of health and medical application categories:

> Alerts and awareness: The best way for a physician to keep up to date is NOT by attending a symposium once a year, or by checking emails. Clinical care is information intensive. Hence, making an up to date, mature mobile source available by Smart Device is the most up-to-date solution. "Epocrates" offers up to date online medical reference sources. 60% of Epocrates users report avoiding 3 or more medical errors a month. Doctors using the referenced Smart Device tool save at least 20 minutes a day in pharmacy call-backs and real-time information searches while in the examination room with the patient.

> "Skyscape" is another medical reference firm. It works with 50 health publishers and has assembled the largest library of medical resources available for every Smart Device operating systems. Like physicians, consumers also access medical information via mobile Devices. The "Evincii" applications helps consumers look for over-the-counter medication for particular symptoms. This application grew out of a service once available in retail pharmacies. The Mayo Clinic's "Symposium Checker" Smart Device application is similar to the hospital's online version.

Diagnostic Tools:

General diagnosis with Smart Devices: Diagnosaurus offers differential diagnosis (uses a process of elimination of causes). IDdx is a Smart Device application covering infectious disease diagnosis based on the Control of Communicable Disease manual. Some Smart Device based diagnostic applications target specific conditions. STAR Analytic Services developed a Smart Device application that analyzes coughs. Coughs are the most common symptom a patient presents.

Smart Device based laboratory applications: Smart Devices can deliver physicians' laboratory and blood work results as soon as they are completed. This just-in-time reporting and help physicians and patients avoid phone tag. If a value is abnormal, the physician can immediately email a patient, with his Smart Device, follow up instructions. The laboratory application will next assist clinicians in interpreting laboratory results and providing diagnostic support. Current popular laboratory applications include ARUP Consult and Care360.

Smart Device based digital imaging: The OsiriX Application can be thought of as a mobile PACS (picture archiving communications system) for the Smart Device. At the recent meeting of the Radiological Society of North America (RSNA), several papers Papers demonstrated the value of using Smart Devices in digital imaging applications. ERoentgen Radiology Dx is an application that helps radiologists identify the most appropriate radiology examination for a patient.

ECGs (electrocardiographs) via Smart Devices: There are many electrocardiogram applications that offer the most common ECG results. Instant ECG (one of the top paid iPhone applications), ECG Guide, and ECG Interpreter are among the most used.

Smart Devices in Emergency Departments: Mobile health solutions on Smart Devices are designed to increase productivity in busy Emergency Rooms. Physicians use Vigilance application to track patients' vital signs, transmit live videos from exam and operating rooms, and receive alerts when patients are in distress so doctors can respond even before nurses page them.

Smart Devices in Obstetrics: AirStrip OB is an iPhone application that provides obstetricians with a real-time, remote access to fetal heart tracings, contraction patterns, nursing notes, and vital signs. Obstetricians can monitor different stages of labor even when they are not by a patient's side. This increases the obstetrician's ongoing interaction with the labor and delivery department and gives doctors real-time data.

Smart Device use for remote physician consultation: These have emerged through services like American Well, Myca Health, RelayHealth, and TelaDoc. These negotiate payment between the payer, provider and patient. Qualcomm is a company with 12,000 employees. They operate a corporate "clinic without walls" using Smart Devices. Using Myca they provide remote health communications between the health center staff and the mobile employees. The head doctor notes that the employees are so connected to their Smart Devices, they keep them on the right health and wellness path.

Continuing Medical Education (CME) provides credits using Smart Devices. Several programs provide CME credits for clinical research done online. CME is provided by Smart Devices using Web browsers with multimedia formats such as Flash. Several services provide CME credits using Smart Devices. Included are Epocrates, Mobile CME, MedPage Today, QuantiaMD, ReachMD, Skyscape CME STAT, and UpTo date. Wolters Kluwer Health developed the

XtraCredit Smart Device application that provides CME credit for clinical research done online.

Patient records applications for Smart Devices are offered by several organizations including: Allscripts, CareTools iChart, eClinicalWorks, EPIC's Haiku, LifeRecord, MacPractice MD, motionPHR, NextGen, Ringful, and Webahn. Using this application, physicians can communicate with patients from anywhere.

Several Smart Device applications are used to track medications. The "Pillboxer Lite" application tracks medications, vitamins, and supplements with a graphic interface that resembles a pill box. "GlowCaps" send information to the drug manufacturer to the doctor. They also remind the user to take the medication with lights and tones. They can automatically order refills.

A number of Smart Device applications connect patients with chronic conditions to clinicians, caregivers and health coaches on a continuous basis. These applications combine sensor technologies with communications. Sensors include accelerometers, infrared detectors, that measure temperatures and glucometers to measure blood sugars. Similar arrangements are used for home care patients, and wellness and fitness applications. These techniques apply also to children and aging patients.

Mobile health is one of the top ten mobile applications with Smart Devices. It helps to reduce costs related to treating diseases and to improve patients' quality of life. The opportunity is that 70% of patients with two or more chronic conditions have a wireless phone. Smart Device use is expected to increase further.

Education:

To some persons, having wireless phones in school can seem to be a distraction. On the contrary, having Smart Devices and Smart Devices in schools can be very helpful. Consider these advantages:

Easy contact: A quick call to home is possible if school ends early. Or, if a health problem requires student pick up. Perhaps, a late pick up at school requires notification to the student.

GPS Tracking: Most Smart Devices include the GPS function. It locates the unit accurately, and the units holder. That function offers a quick safety check on a child's location. It also helps to track a lost or misplaced unit.

School work facilitator: Discussion with another student helps to clarify a home work assignment. Access to the Internet and services such as Google facilitate research to respond to assigned questions. Calls to a parent enable adjusting joint study times. Access to lectures and conferences facilitates learning. Use of email and the Internet prepares the student for daily life skills. The Internet also enables direct access to libraries and ebook reading units, maps, graphics drawings, news, gaming programs, TV, motion pictures and text books.

Emergency help: Smart Devices give direct access to organizations which provide assistance such as the AAA (the American Automobile Association) and the AARP (American Association of retired Persons). Perhaps, more important, the Smart Device allows talking directly to emergency personnel before they can physically arrive at the scene of an emergency. Those can be very important minutes of assistance until help physically arrives. Use of the Smart Device can also quickly get additional unplanned assistance.

These considerations raise an important question. At what age should a child get a Smart Device ? Today, more than 75% of children 12 to 17 years old have a wireless phone. They have no difficulty using the wireless phone.

There are a large number of Smart Device education oriented applications available on the Internet. Look at "101bestandroidapps.com". It covers the education role from learning the alphabet to memory training. These applications are also useful in areas other than formal education.

E-Post Letters:

This is a new service offered by the Deutsche Post. The details are not yet available but it is expected to be a Smart Device activated service. The service offers to deliver an e-mail message to those without e-mail access. The service prints an e-mail message. The message is put into a stamped envelope and delivered by the snail (conventional) mail delivery system, at the same price as a conventional stamped envelope. The United States, British and Swiss postal systems are reported as experimenting with the same offering. The real issue is that conventional postage volumes are shrinking and this application is claimed to be more secure than conventional mail or e-mail systems. The E-Post offering allows the postal systems to participate in the growing use of e-mail.

Protecting Children on Smart Devices:

Several applications monitor the voice content looking for keywords such as "drugs" and "suicide", to or from the Smart Device. They also set up GPS controlled geographic "no-text" zones to prevent the phones being used in school environments to cheat on tests or to taunt classmates. The programs are offered by Kids Phone Advocate, Pueblo West, Colorado and WebSafety, Irving, Texas. Both units send alerts as emails or text messages to the parent's computer and phones. They do require a Smart Device with data plans. Both offerings also have a feature to disable the Smart Device's ability to send or receive text message when in a vehicle going faster than 10 miles per hour. It is intended to curb testing while driving. The feature can be unlocked by the parent when the child is a passenger. The basic products are $ 9.99 per month. The WebSafety mobile product costs $ 9.99 a month for one Smart Device or $ 39.99 a month for an unlimited number of Smart Devices.

Smart Device as a Credit Card Terminal:

The "Squares Up" system provides a magnetic striped, card-swiping card reader that plugs into the Smart Device's headphone jack. The Square plug-in is free. Each transaction is charged 2.75 percent of the total transaction value, plus $0.15. To become a credit card accepting merchant requires a one or two year contract, at $ 15 to $ 25 per month with a minimum transaction fees of $ 25 per month. The "Square" Company is in San Francisco.

There are two other offerings similar to Square. They are FocusPay and Intuit's GoPayment. They both offer a Smart Device application and a magnetic stripe reader that attaches through the Smart Device or Tablet audio circuit orifice. In each case the application is activated, the magnetic stripe reader is installed, the audio volume is turned to maximum on, and the magnetic stripe is swiped for reading. The application software takes the use of the stripe content from there to create an input transaction and the appropriate records, including ledger entries and receipts to the card holder.

All of the magnetic stripe card reading applications have the same weaknesses. A loss or stolen Smart Device provides the thief with a full capability as well as access to your value accounts. PIN values are available through PIN recall application facilities. Message copy allows multiple repeat entries. Ease of access does not provide effective security.

Smart Device Based Wagering:

Smart Device application enables Nevada, USA, gamblers to place bets within the State. American Wagering, Inc, operates 60 sports books in the state. The better must initially appear in person to create an account and load the application. The Smart Device requires the GPS function which is tested to prove the better is within the state when placing a wager. The better does not have to be at the book to bet. It is expected that similar applications will be made available for the other major betting firms in the state.

Smart Device Based Company Stores:

Companies are creating in-house Smart Device application stores for employees. The stores are intended to provide applications that help the employees get their work done. The applications cover an extensive range from scheduling conference rooms to approving purchasing orders. Forrester Research is forecasting that by 2015 half of all Devices on US corporate networks will be mobile units. Companies having these facilities include IBM, Google and Apple. Other corporate programs are used to distribute the applications, to impose security requirements and also to wipe the programs off a Smart Device Device when the employee leaves the company. The companies invite employees to write their own applications and download them to the company store. (I would assume some form of quality control is imposed on those application programs).

Smart Device Based Diabetes Control:

Baltimore based WellDoc's has a FDApproved Smart Device application for managing diabetes. The application allows the user to enter their blood sugar test readings into their Smart Device. The application program is being distributed by AT&T to 1.2 million employees, retirees and their dependents. The application responds to the blood sugar reading entry with real-time feedback on what they should eat and other ways they can help to stabilize their blood sugar. The Smart Device application can also alert users when they need to test their blood sugar level. The application also sends the date to the application vendor's server for further analysis. It can then be assessed by he user's physicians and disease management caseworkers.

It can also support glucose meters that can send data via Bluetooth wireless technology. (ref: Health Data Management, 12/10, page 10).

Citi Bank Introduces the Citi Shopper (citishopper.citi.com):

The free, down loadable, application allows the GPS based service from Smart Devices. The consumers input the name of a product they want to acquire. The response s the name of the closest retailers selling that product, along with a map. They are also testing a sticker with PayPass technology. They can be used at some 230,000 merchant outlets, world wide. The contactless stickers can be used to make payments. The stickers are used only with MasterCards. Contact Citi Senior VP Kurt. Weiss@citi.com.

Social networks and Mobile Devices

Social networks bring together people and the content they create and share. They are a dynamic ecosystem that incubates and nurtures relationships between people and the content they create and share. Google lists more than 100 such networks. They vary by common subject, geographic location, language used and goals. Almost all social networks thrive on the Internet. Hence, the Smart Device becomes the instrument of Social Networks' communication with its Internet interface and a broad set of application programs to speed participation.

Three of the largest social networks are Facebook, Twitter and Linkedin. Facebook, for example has 700 million active users, 50 % of which log in on any given day. The average user has 130 friends. 70% of the users are outside the United States. 200 million active members access Facebook through their mobile Device. Mobile user are twice as active as non-mobile users. There are more than 200 mobile operators in 60 countries working to deploy and promote Facebook mobile products. These include:

Facebook.com: works on all phones with mobile web

Access. They text link to your Smart Device. They update your status, browse your news feed and view friends' profiles.

Facebook Text Messages: Update your status and message friends using text messages. Receive SMS texts with status updates, messages and wall posts, as they happen.

Facebook for your phone: Download rich, interactive applications built for your specific Smart Device.

Smart Device Based Stock Trading

Speed of action can be a vital function in stock trading. Trading in public stocks requires current information about the market status of a stock and related market news. The ability of a Smart Device to receive current news and telephone reports makes it a valuable tool in active stock trading. Stock trading requires these steps:

1. Establish a trading service relationship.
   Here are three made-for-mobile trading services:

   Charles Schwab: pb.schwab.com

   E-Trade: wireless.etrade.com   TD Ameritrade: amtdw. com

2. Receive stock quotes directly on your Smart Device:

   BusinessWeek: businessweek.mobi
   CNNMoney: cnnmoney.mobi Quote.com: quote.mobi

3. Arrange to make payments with your Smart Device.

   PayPal: paypal.com (via NFC)
   Obopay (mobile): obopay.com

The Smart Device offers a solution to a time-sensitive application requirement of stock trading.

Mobile Search:

There are hundreds of thousands of Internet sites. The number is increasing fast. How do you keep track ? How do you find the information you are looking for ? The answer is that you use mobile search services. Although they are a free service, there may be carrier service fees associated with the Smart Device operation. Check this possibility first.

There are several search programs to select:

Google	google.mobi
Microsoft live Search:	m.live.com
Yahoo! oneSearch:	yahoo.mobi
Find.mobi:	find.mobi

Most search engines have similar user interfaces. Your challenge is to specify your search objectives as clearly as possible. Consider these guides in formulating your search request:

Use short but concise terms: For example, I want a bus in New York. A more effective search criteria would be: New york bus

Identify some local or regional element, such as a location name.

If possible, use the search engine that has given you the best result for a like query.

The made-for-mobile web page is different. For example:

Mobile web pages are smaller. They don't contain as many words. Be more selective in use of terms.

Mobile web pages are less linked because of their smaller size. Focus on their content.

>   Mobile search is for mobile users. Use more caution in term selection and response evaluation.
>
>   Consider using regular search units for more in-depth analysis.

Although mobile Internet sites are smaller, being able to make a basic search with your Smart Device can be a real time saver. Use these guides to improve your search results.

Device Fingerprinting

Device fingerprinting is a relatively new science. It identifies inanimate objects by their properties. For example, a desk computer would be identified by these characteristics: screen size, fonts used, browser used, and operating system. The concept is being developed by BlueCava. One major use is to use the fingerprint to target users of mobile Devices for advertising of mobile Device offerings. The concept is being tested by Mobext, the US cellphone advertising arm of the French firm Havas, SA. Be prepared for a more intense advertising campaign aimed at your Smart Device.

Conclusion:

Mobile Smart Device based marketing applications are relatively new in the United States. However, their use goes back more than ten years in Asia. The real challenge is for the United States market to catch up. With more than 450,000 applications available for some Smart Devices, your challenge will be to selectively use those that benefit your use and goals for your Smart Device.

Chapter iii-5

Unbanked, Under Banked and the Internet.

Purpose: To describe two major customer sets, whose banking actions are not generally understood.

Action: Use these descriptions to evaluate your plan for these customer sets.

Introduction

Unbanked refers to any household or individual that does not make use of a financial institution for any type of financial or banking service or transaction. Under banked are small businesses with access to financial services but do not use them. The Unbanked are reported as 10% of USA population. Under banked are reported at an additional 15% of he USA population. These are currently reported as 28 million plus 45 million people. Both groups, the Unbanked and Under banked, spend $130 million per year on alternative but relatively expensive financial services. These include check cashing services, pay day loans and money transfer services. Both have been seen as future business opportunities by most bankers.

In the United States the unbanked group tends to be younger, single and in lower income groups. They tend to be more women, with the group having less education. While some have attended college, they are less likely to be college graduates. They are less likely to have children and tend to be ethnics (minorities).

Credit cards are an important option for the Unbanked. Banks tend to aggressively sell them to the young age group. The applications tend to be available on campuses. Prepaid transaction cards and Prepaid Smart Devices are also attractive to this group. Check cashing is expensive for this group and is used by a smaller portion.

The Under Banked

The under banked use a number of non bank products. They include non bank financial products. They including payday loans, pawn shops, rent to own, and refund anticipation loans. The under banked use these products because they are easier to get than bank loans.

The Internet

One third of the Unbanked consumers use Smart Devices on the Internet. That is about half of the banked consumers, percentage wise. The Unbanked use the Internet as follows:

E-mail:	69% Online Unbanked Consumers
Weather	35%
News	35%
Job Search	22%
Movie Listings	20%

The specific Internet applications which are more attractive to the Unbanked than to the average Internet user include games (7% more), employment search (11% more) and online dating (63% more).

During a typical month, the Unbanked visited these web sites:

Yahoo	42% of Online Unbanked
Google 32% eBay	17%
MapQuest	17%
AOL	16%

During the past year, the percentage of online Unbanked consumers made these Internet based purchases:

Clothing	14% of Online Unbanked
Books	14%
CD's, Tapes Other music	9%
Groceries	9%
Airline tickets	9%

The locations from which the Unbanked access the Internet include:

Home	56% of Online Unbanked
	(34% less than Banked)
Public libraries	85%
Schools	37%

Reaching Hispanic Market

Thirty five per cent of the Unbanked American population are Hispanic. Hispanic consumers are nearly three times as likely as the average adult to be Unbanked. They tend to be 10 years younger the overall market. 52% of the American Hispanic market are foreign born. As Hispanics grow older they accumulate wealth and do become banked customers. Targeting the Unbanked Hispanics is generally done with a store-within-a-store strategy. Walmart has 50% of the Unbanked attracted by this arrangement.

Using Credit to Attract the Unbanked

A Texas financial services firm (Progressive Finance) has booths in 140 grocery stores. They make uncollateralized loans of $ 350 to $ 2,500. The loss rate on the portfolio is under 10%, even though 55% of their clients have no credit history.

Unbanked, An African Example:

Local banks charge a fee for saving small amounts which discourages savings. A new financial service in Kenya, called M-PESA, lets people use their mobile Devices to transfer small amounts. The service also creates a digital wallet to hold the funds until needed. Thus, the mobile Device wallet becomes a savings Device until the funds are needed. It is forecast that by 2012, .7 billion of the unbanked poor will have a $20 mobile Device. In Kenya, 70% of the country's adults have an M-PESAccount, which can also be used to pay bills or send cash by texting. There are now 100 services like M-PESA. Banks in Kenya have tried to compete with a service called M-KESHO. It has high fees for deposits and withdrawals. It has only been accepted by 5% of the accounts compared to M-PESA. (Businessweek, 9/12/11, pages 55/56).

Conclusion

The Unbanked consumer can be reached via the Internet. While their big ticket purchases trail those of the general market there are some categories, such as electronics, which are stand-out for the Unbanked. Further, retailer financing packages profit from creating plans for the unbanked. Bankers will need to seek new approaches to this potentially valuable market. Perhaps, a low cost, pre paid smart Device or Smart Device based product will be an attractive toll for this group.

Reference:

www.scarborough.com

Chapter iii-6

Micro Payments and The Internet

Purpose: Understanding Smart Device based micro payment alternatives.

Action: Evaluate your potential role. Assign responsibility.

Introduction

A remarkable characteristic of the Internet is the amount of free material available to anyone. Some providers, like Google, have evolved a plan to get advertisers to pay for the free results provided to its users. That is very much like the payment by advertisers for free radio broadcast programs which clearly identify the sponsor. However, it is expected that some web providers in the future will expect payment for their content. Bank services are paid for by the bank's customers in the form of loan and mortgage payments and the use of deposits. However, future bank services may need transaction payment amounts which are smaller in value. Similarly, Internet providers will need to avail themselves of techniques for collecting a larger volume of smaller amounts in payments.

A promising method for implementing small amount payment and collection is called a "micro payment". These Smart Device transactions may be as small as a fraction of a dollar, or the local currency. These payments offer more than payment. They also offer the opportunity to deal in Smart Device based smaller "micro-loans". They open the opportunity for the Internet to "efficiently" deal in smaller transactions, such as transit, tolls, and payment for shorter information packet's such as booklets and smaller, more specialized newspapers.

There will continue to be free Internet products and services. However, the growing involvement of the Smart Device based Internet transactions in the everyday activities of life will require that paying for the lower end of the value spectrum of Internet offerings will be essential.

Micro Payment Efforts To Date

There have been a number of unsuccessful micro payment efforts to date. There have been two types. One type is so complex to implement that it discourages use. The second type is so simple that it is easily compromised by counterfeiting or other attacks. The first generation micro payment systems occurred in the mid 1990's.These were eCash, CyberCom and MilliCent. They disappeared slowly in the late 1990's. The second generation of micro payments appeared in the late 1990's.

Micro Payments Technical Characteristics

A "token" is an encrypted string of bits used to represent monetary value. A micro payment is a "low" value payment scheme which may be Smart Device based. The micro payment scheme has these technical components:

> The micro payment scheme has a basic token or e-coin used for value exchange. The user buys tokens from a broker to use to pay a merchant via his Smart Device. The merchant sends his received tokens to his broker. His broker then transfers the equivalent monetary value to the merchant's account.
>
> The design of the micro payment scheme has these technical characteristics:
>
> Ease of use.
>
> Allows customers to be anonymous.
>
> Merchants are never anonymous
>
> Provided by a micro payment operator (MPSO)

Scalable to increasing volume without p e r f o r m a n c e degradation.

Validation provided by:

On-line: by a third party
Semi On-line—for some payments
Off-line: without a third party.

Security for non-repudiation (non denial)

Authentication
Authorization
Data Integrity
Confidentiality

May have Inter operability

Paid by users of another system
Requires rules standardization
Provides currency convertibility.

The micro payment scheme has these non technical characteristics:

Trust: The user knows the MPSO bears risks.

Security technology increases the trust users feel.

Coverage: Percent of merchants and customers that can use the payment system. (Sometimes called Acceptance and Penetration).

Privacy: Protection of personal and payment information.

Prepaid: Customer transfers money to system before using micro payments.

Postpaid: Customer makes micro payment and pays later.

Range of Payments: Minimum and maximum payment values supported, including Smart Devices.

Multicurrency: Supported?

There were two types of early Micro Payment systems:

Token based: Millicent, Ecash, Micromint, Pay Word, and Net Cash.

Account based: Mondex, Cybercoin, and Mini-Pay

They were:

Use complicated, non anonymous, limited scalability, and on-line validation.

Variety of security—most not fully secure.

No inter operability.

Did not prove trustworthy.

Low coverage.

Majority were prepaid.

Most used US dollars.

None multicurrency, some usable in several countries. The second generation micro payment systems were: Mostly account based with easier administration.

Generally required two or three simple interactions with customer to process payments. Customer provides account number. Receives receipt. Merchant receives a confirmation.

Ease of use—a big improvement. Most used a Web interface. Accessible from anywhere.

Anonymity: Allows customer anonymity.

Scalability: Most account based.

Validation: Provided on-line via the Internet. Considered more trustworthy and secure.

Security—Most use HTTP Web protocol.

> Requires authentication of communicating partners.

> Encrypts and decrypts data.

> Supported by all Browsers.

> Generates information to prevent non repudiation.

> Allows tracing back and verifying payments.

> Product delivery issues directly between customer and merchant.

Inter operability: Not solved. No micro payment standards.

Trust: Increased significantly by legislation.

Bank involvement is a major help.

Coverage: High. Most customers accustomed to working with the Internet.

Privacy: MPSO's support plus legislation.

Prepaid: Most. Limits fraud. Few post paid. Requires long term contracts.

Range of payments, multicurrency: Varies a lot.

Most support one currency.

Summary:

Most second generation micro payment solutions give increased coverage; are convenient; user friendly; adequate security; a high degree of anonymity; faster; but low standardization. Most deploy proprietary solutions. Inter operabilty is solved using Smart Devices.

In the future, solutions will merge and there will be just a few, like the credit card business.

Reference: www.springerlink.com/index/8u72715711003x3.pdf

Chapter iii-7

Who is Who in Smart Device Based Mobile Banking

Purpose: Identify the key software providers

Action: Use the list to contact software sources.

This is a list of software suppliers at the time this report was prepared. It is important to repeat a search of the Internet for the most recent list when you are preparing to use this information. This is a fast moving industry. Only the most current of search results will provide you with a current list of software suppliers.

Organization	eMail	Specialty
CASI Software	casisoft.com	IBM mainframe

> IBM main frame information transformation and delivery solutions. Outbound delivery via email, SMS messaging or Web browser.

ClairMail	clairmail.com	2 way banking mobile

> A two-way mobile solution for banking, payments and card services through actionable alerts, workflows and personalized touch across multiple mobile channels.

Clickatell   clickatell.comfinancial.php   digital bankingservices

Customers can pay bills, transfer funds or make deposits via the mobile Smart Device. Delivers a flexible platform that enables banks to offer tailored digital bankingservice to customers.

CPNI   cpni-inc.com   mobile payments

Phone authorized transfer mobile payment solutions. Global mobile payment message routing; customers download bank-branded Java application to their mobile Smart Devices.

Firethorn Hldgs   firethornmobile.com   mobile transactions

Mobil transaction services. Enables consumers to securely perform a wide variety of banking and payment functions any time, using their mobile Smart Device, PDA or other mobile Devices.

FIS   fidelityinfoservices.com/fnfis   mobile financial services

Mobile card downloadable application with balance inquiry, intra-card transfer, mini-statements; browser access to application; iPhone application in App store; mobile bill pay with standard bill pay viewing, scheduling, changing, canceling and expedited bill pay.

Fiserv   fiserv.com   mobile money

Mobile money and mobile money fast track are available in an in-house or hosted version. The Triple Play technology supports the three primary mobile access modes—mobile browser, SMS and downloaded application—through a single platform.

Fronde Anywhere　　　frondeanywhere.com　mobile payment

Mobile payment and security solutions for banks, payment providers and mobile operators. The Anywhere platform delivers secure mobile banking, payment and security services from a single system.

Fundamo　　　　　fundamo.com　　　applications

Applications for banks, mobile operators, third-party payment processors and other enterprises with SMS, Web browser, use of SIM card in GSM handsets for security.

Gemalto　　　gemalto.com/financial　　hosted services

A secure service platform that communicates with the end user via mobile operator, safeguarding customer Information through end-to-end encryption. The financial institution controls the user experience and security throughout the entire process. The NFC ecosystem can link any bank with any mobile Device on any operator's network providing end-to-end security.

IBM　　Ibm.com/industries/financial services/us/index　Systems

Hardware, software, partners and assets for system integration and hosting for mobile commerce solutions, be they digital banking or mobile payments.

Jack Henry Assoc's　jackhenry.com　　　Mobile Offerings

Users can conduct typical in-branch and online transactions. Supports all account types. Also, will enable users to initiate bank-to-bank funds transfers, receive alerts and make mobile payments.

M-Com Inc   m-com.us   BankAnywhere

> Digital banking and payments platform for credit unions, retail and commercial banks. Includes back-end capabilities such as enrollment channels, reporting, fraud monitoring and reporting.

mFoundry   mfoundry.com   Three Mode Mobile Banking

> Integrated mobile applications including native support for iPhone and iPod. One integrated solution for consistent brand experience across all modes and no need to integrate with multiple vendors.

Mobile Money   Ventures mmventures.com   Mobile Apps

> A customizable platform for delivering the next generation of mobile finance, including banking payments, stock trading, deals and rewards.

Montise PLC   monitise.com   Payments Processors

> Digital banking and payments network; digital banking and payments ecosystem.

MShift   mshift.com   Mobile Banking

Browser-based/mobile web interface; SMS for real-time alerts. WAP (wireless application protocol)-based.

Obopay   obopay.com   Mobile Money

> P2P payments; lets consumers and businesses purchase, pay and transfer money through any mobile Device.

Pyxis Mobile   pyxismobile.com   Mobile Applications

> Retail banking mobile applications to access accounts, transfer funds, manage payments and investments, and access real-time market data/news.

Research in Motion   rim.net   Wireless Platform

> The BlackBerry wireless platform enables carriers, financial institutions and vendors to deliver digital bankingsolutions to their customers.

S1 postillion.com   s1.com   Postillion Banking

> Postillion (one who rides the lead horse) mobile banking. Consumer and small business-focused banking and payments functionally available on a mobile browser or SMS Devices.

Sprint   sprint.com/finance   Mobile Loan

> Mobile loan office, my MoneyManager. Sprint nationwide PCS network.

Sybase 365   sybase.com/365   End-to-End

> An end-to-end solution for mBanking, mPayments, and mRemittance, designed for mobile operators and financial institutions. Enables financial institutions to interact with customers in real time through mobile alerts, two way banking and payment services.

Telrock   telrock.com   TextDebit

> TextDebits mobile payment system; TextRequest account management; self account management through mobile Device.

Tyfone, Inc.   tyfone.com   Secure Memory Card

Secure memory card based mobile banking, mobile contactless payments, mobile remittance and microfinance, mobil identity management, mobile retail loyalty and remote payments.

VeriSign   verisign.com   Flexible Solution

Allows banks and financial institutions to provide their customers with convenient, on-the-go access to banking and other financial services. These include one-way services such as withdrawal alerts, checking and salary deposit confirmation, account statements, and credit card transaction alerts, and two-way interactive services such as balance inquiries, bill payments and funds transfers, via the mobile Device.

Yodlee   yodlee.com   Personal Financial   Mgmt

Portfolio of comprehensive personal financial management payments and alerts service via online and mobile channels.

It is important to do a further search on the Internet when examining the possible sources of applicable application programs available for Smart Devices and other mobile Devices.

(ref: Bank Systems and Technology)

IV Smart Devices and New Markets

Chapter iv-1

Tablets and other Smart Device
Functions and Features

Purpose: Describe available options.

Action: Choose the functions you require.

Introduction

Mobile is a three legged stool. The three legs are the laptop, the smart Device and the tablet. Stools offer stability for mobility. Laptops are best for content creation. Smart Devices are great for messaging and talking. Tablets are best for reviewing and showing it to others. However, in the final analysis the results are a function of your experience.

Smart Device Operating Systems

An Operating System is a software program that runs on a computer and manages the computer components. It provides common services needed for efficient execution of application software. With application functions such as input, output, and memory allocation, the operating system acts as an intermediary between the application program (software) and the computer hardware.

The major Smart Device operating systems for Mobile Web and application usage are:

iPhone 4 3% Apple, AT&T

Symbian 36% Used on more than 100 Smart Devices

RIM   9% Balckberry and Verizon

Windows 5% Mobile

Android 3% Google developed based on Linux

Palm   2% Also called Garnet Operating System

Other   2%

Radio-Frequency Identification Devices (RFID)

Radio-Frequency identification Devices (RFID) use an antenna to receive a radio signal carrying data and, possibly, electric power. The signal is processed by an integrated circuit Device. The received signal identifies the source and inquires of the integrated circuit identification. The response is transmitted back via the antenna to the remote inquiry unit. In some cases, the received signal may also include power to energize the RFID unit. In other examples, the RFID unit may include a battery for power. There are a broad array of applications for RFID tags from automatic toll systems, to banking data capture and access control and security identification. RFID-like function may be added to existing smart Devices with a "sticker" carried RFID circuit.

The Changing Smart Device Spectrum: Tablets

As with any fast growing technology product area, the Smart Device is inviting the development of product variations and improvements. A good example is the development of "Tablet" Devices which include Smart Device functions. The tablet is a middle ground between the handheld Smart Device and the laptop computer. It has a 10 inch (diagonal) screen with "Touch Screen" response. The tablet allows a set of applications whose parameters exceed the capacity of a Smart Device. This includes document display, e-Book display facility, writing and editing of documents, a "virtual" keyboard (displayed), and photograph viewing. In addition, it offers the normal variety of Smart Device applications. Some tablets offer conventional smart Device facility together with wireless access. The tablet is too large to fit in a shirt pocket. It usually does fit in a coat pocket. Migration to a tablet size Smart Device opens several new Device applications, as follows:

> TV Content: The added display area permits viewing of TV formatted information. This may be pay TV or free TV, depending on the material source.

> e-Book: The screen size allows displaying full size book pages. It has much of the look and feel of print on paper. E-Books in the United States vary, as follows:

>> Prices: From $ 79 to $ 489 (Amazon Kindle).

>> Screens: From 6 inches to 9.7 inches (Kindle).

>> Downloads: US 3G, Wi-Fi, and International 3G

>> Available books: Google (over 1 million), to Amazon (over 360,000).

> Touch technology: Two types are available. A multilayer Resistive technology and a Capacitive technology using human body's electrical characteristics.

Some people prefer physical books. It is yours forever. You can access a book any time you want. Some e-Book providers limit the number of times you can down load an e-book content. The best resolution is to down load the e-Book content to your Personal Computer (PC). When you want to read the e-Book content transfer the e-Book content via USB connection to any e-Book of your choice. That will only work for Amazon's Kindle.

You can access thousands of e-Book contents from Project Guttenberg (pcworld.com/63480). This is a collaborative project of the University of North Carolina. It covers a broad array of information types, including software, music, literature, art, history and science. The content of Project Guttenberg is also visible on your Smart Device, not just Kindle. Feedbooks (feedbooks.com) is another good source of e-Book content. If the content is not Kindle compatible, you can convert the contents with

Calibre (find. pcworld.com/63479). This program can also be used to manage your library content and synchronize your books content.

iPads to Replace Laptops

Access to internal corporate programs with iPad use is available with a free application program from Citrix Systems, Inc. The iPad also runs the same software as the iPhone with a number of business-friendly applications. The iPads, with list prices of $ 429 to $ 829 are less expensive than laptop computers. In addition, the iPads provide better demonstrations, start more quickly and have longer lasting batteries. Their Pads have performed well with industry Specialized applications. They have performed well in medical applications for viewing medical images such as X-Rays and CT Scans. The iPads are also better for accessing medical records. iPads have been used in hotels by concierges because of their ease in mobile use. The iPads have given construction managers mobile access to construction drawings and related support materials in the field.

Developer Datawind in India has joined many India companies that offer the world's least expensive innovations, such as a $ 2,000 car and $ 2,000 open heart surgery. Datawind is selling tablets for $ 45 each. With government subsidies, students will get the units for $ 35. They expect to produce 100,000 units a month. They had attempted to produce a $ 10 computer, but did not succeed. (SJ Mercury News from AP).

Chapter iv-2

Mobile Applications Around the World for Smart Phones

Purpose: Identify major international applications.

Action: Select those of value.

Vodafone Mobile Recording (UK) (enterprise.vodafone.com):

Records and archives mobile calls, voicemails and text messages. Compatible with Smart Devices including Blackberry's.

Turkcall Mobile payments for Micropayments (Turkey) (turkcell.com.tr):

Makes micropayments for amounts under 17 Euros. Users exceed 1 million (compared to 22 million credit cards users). Solution offered for the unbanked.

Tatra Banka (Slovakian Market)

(itunes/apple.com/us/app/tatra-banka):

Accessible through the iTunes store. Accesses accounts and credit cards. Provides map of branches and ATM's. Provides table of exchange rates. Offers authentication and authorization with encrypted online banking transactions. Provides "QuickPay" for automatic bill payment.

T Smart Wallet (Korea) (smartwallet.co.kr):

Replaces a physical wallet filled with plastic cards, paper coupons, credit cards and cash. Allows storage and usage through mobile Smart Devices. Now used by 25 million customers of SK Tellecom, Korea. Downloaded via mobile Internet (URL) to mobile Smart Devices. Currently limited to Android/Windows mobile Smart Devices. Users can set password access to applications to prevent unauthorized use. Reported lost or stolen Smart Devices can be shut down. Extensive us of partnering with other card issuers. Processes global bar code standards.

Scotia Digital banking(21 Countries) (scotiabank.com/mobilebanking/appl):

Offers realtime banking services via Smart Devices. Over 175 K active customers averaging 2 million transactions per month. Integrated GPS based branch and ATM locations. Available with most Smart Devices as a free service. Processing requests with almost 100% availability and within 2 seconds.

Santanda Rio Digital banking(Argentina):

Offers location based information (branch and ATM's) and digital bankingtransactions. Offers shopping discounts, shop locations and driving directions. Operates with Blackberry's, iPhones and 80% of available Smart Devices.

Orange Cityzi Pass (Nice, France)(orange.cityzi.fr):

Mobile Smart Device services. First multiserver provider in Europe. Uses NFC touch point for daily transactions, loyalty coupons, store card services and bus ticketing with real time bus schedule access. Free until June 2016. Blocks service for loss or stolen units.

m-park (Tallinn, Estonia)(pargi.ee):

Enables mobile payment for parking services. 90% of all parking are paid by mobile Device and appear on the mobile Device bills. Provides numerous payment options. Easy implementation.

Hana N Money (Korea) (hanabank.com):

A Personal Finance Management application with asset management and mobile coupon service. Includes asset management and coupons on maps. A free application with more than 2 million users. An extensive security architecture includes three security and anti-virus modules with digital certificates to shut out hacking. The coupon offers include current map locations. The application is preinstalled on Samsung Smart Devices.

PlatiMo (Mobile Pay in Serbian)

(telenor.rs/en/consumer/services/platimo/):

A payment service for 69 banks and 3 million subscribers. It enable payments from the consumer's bank using his mobile Device. It uses a PIN code for payment confirmation. Transactions are secured with end-to-end encryption. The application works on most Smart Devices.

GCASH REMIT (17 countries) (globe.com.ph/gcash):

A low value, cash oriented transaction service. It offers mobile money transfers in small stores. It now serves 30,000 customers on a monthly basis. It serves "micro-entrepreneurs" with a minimum investment.

GCASH CARD (a companion to GCASH REMIT):

Offers access to a Smart Device based mobile wallet through 9000 ATM's in the Philippines. Access is available on a 24/7 basis. The withdrawal service is PIN based.

Easypaisa (Pakistan)((easypaisa.com.pk):

Offers branchless banking at more than 12,000 retail points across Pakistan Provides no paperwork money transfers. One third of transactions are in rural areas. Only 7% of the population have bank accounts. The system allows secure bill payment and money transfers.

BOKU (65 countries) (boku.com):

Offers multiple payment options including PayPal, credit cards, and BOKU. BOKU is an Android application for Smart Devices. The system works with 220 mobile carriers worldwide. Serves under banked personnel with, potentially, 3 billion consumers. The security system provides a double authorization process based on the mobile account number and physical possession of the mobile Device.

BilltoMobile (US markets) (billtomobile.com):

Allows purchase of goods and services to be billed directly to the mobile account. Danal Co, a Korean company provides the service. It is now available to 65% of the US population (185 million potential subscribers). It has processed $ 4 billion in online transactions for 185,000 users at more than 10,000 global merchants. No pre-registration is needed. A purchase takes 10 to 15 seconds. They deliver low cost secure payments through 16 carriers. By the end of 2016 they expect to cover 95% of US subscribers. They meet all MMA Mobile Marketing Association guidelines.

BonuslaAvea (Turkey) (bonuslaavea.com):

This is the "Avea Mobile Wallet with Bonus". This is a NFC based mobile Device service, where the NFC function need not be built in to the Smart Device. The NFC function is provided by a NFC based SIM card. Card functions include payment and loyalty card options. Services were developed in cooperation with MasterCard.

Airtel (India, Kenyand 4 neighboring East African countries) (airtel.com):

Zap cards from Airtel Africa has 3.2 million customers. The Zap card is a password secured SIM which issues single-use debit card numbers for the Standard Chartered Bank. The one-time virtual cards are made available to mobile Devices. The funds are then deducted with successful completion of a transaction. The one-time password based virtual cards can not be physically stolen or re-used. The number of allowed transactions can be preset. The cards are fully compliant with globally accepted MasterCard processes. This is deliverable to an existing 200 million customers across Africand Asia.

FaceCash (Initially Northern California, USA)(facecash.com):

An application for BlackBerry's, iPhones and Android Smart Devices. The application stores credit card and bank account data. For security it stores a user's photo with a password protected account information and a bar code. The bar code is scanned at a point-of-sale Device. It returns a photo which the clerk compares to the card presenter. The merchant needs a computer (available for $ 150) and a scanner (available for $ 30). The transaction charge is 1.5% of the transaction value. That compares to a credit card authorization charge of about 3.2%. The process is currently debit based, but a bank could also make it credit based transaction. There is no capture of the Smart Device presented picture. (Comment: Busy check out clerks have been known to make poor face/photo comparisons. Is it possible to program the Smart Device to show a different photo than the application returned photo ?).

Chapter iv-3

Smart Devices and Cloud Computing

Purpose: Cloud computing will emerge as a major form of Smart Device based data processing and data base management. These are the basics for an understanding.

Action: How will Cloud process management be established and its integrated with current management practices? How will the transition be managed ?

Introduction

Smart Device based Cloud computing is the delivery of common Smart Device based bank business computer applications from a remote facility, online, through the Internet. These Smart Device based applications are accessed with a Web Browser. It uses software and data stored on servers (computer subsystems). The bank Cloud user rents the Cloud infrastructure from a third party. These Smart Device based Cloud processes reduce cost to the bank user by sharing the Cloud computer power and resources with other users. The user does not have to provide added capacities for peak loads. The user must be concerned about the security of Cloud stored information and its protection to, in and from the Cloud.

Use of Cloud computing with Smart Devices has a low entry cost with little or no upfront costs. Use of high speed band width allows receiving bank application results with the same response time as a local, central dedicated facility. However, the Cloud user pays only for actual processing consumption. Cloud and Smart Device based computing use provides access to a broad range of Smart Device based applications, with significant economic savings opportunities.

History

The Cloud computing concept originated in the 1960's. The term Cloud came into use in the 1990's. It was used to refer to Asynchronous Transfer Mode (ATM) networks. The first commercial attempt in 1999 offered Application Service Providers (ASP's). The early 2000's included the concept in Microsoft's extension to the development of Web services. IBM detailed the concept in 2002 in their "Autonomic Computing Manifesto".

Amazon modernized their data center in 2005. It was designed to get better use of their computer capacity. They provided user's access through Amazon's Web services. In 2007 Google, IBM and a number of universities started a successful large scale Cloud computing research project. In mid 1980, Gartner observed that the change from company owned hardware and software assets to per-use, service-based Cloud based models that appeared practical. Thus, the shift to Cloud computing had started.

In 2009, financial institutions were under intense pressure to cut costs. They were attracted to Cloud computing because its capital expenditures were minimal, support costs were low end and applications, including Smart Devices, could be bought to market relatively quickly. Cloud computing removes the responsibilities of installing, upagerading and maintaining the Smart Device's support computers.

Key Characteristics

Cloud users do not generally own their physical infrastructure. Users avoid capital expenditures by renting computer usage from a third party. Users consume resources as a service. They pay only for the resources they use. Sharing processing power among multiple tenants improves usage rates. It also improves server use by not leaving idle capacities. As combined Cloud usage grows, users do not have to plan for peak loads.

Use of high-speed Cloud based bandwidth communications offers the same response times as a bank located local infrastructure.

Architecture

Most Cloud infrastructures deliver service through datacenters using virtualization technology via the Web. (A virtual machine is simulation of a physical machine. Virtualization is the process of creating virtual machines). The Cloud services are accessible from any point with Internet access, including Smart Device based access. Cloud infrastructures appear on the Internet as a single access point for all of the user's computing needs. Open standards are essential to cloud computing. Open source software provides the basis for many Cloud computing implementations. (A standard is a community agreed definition. Open source is public domain software that allows user to use, change and improve it without constraint).

Types of Cloud Computing

Public or External Cloud is the traditional type. Its resources are provided on a self service basis via the Internet. It uses Web applications, Smart Device access and Web services. It comes from an off-site, third-party source who shares resources. It is billed on a utility-like basis.

Hybrid Cloud uses multiple internal and/or external sources. It combines a local Device, such as a compatible computer, a server, router, Smart Devices or similar hardware and a network interface to a Public Cloud. The interface acts as a firewall and/or spam filter. These are important elements of a secure Cloud and Smart Device based architecture.

Private Cloud uses systems that provide Cloud and Smart Device based functions on a private network. These solutions offer advantages with data security, managed governance and higher reliability solutions. The user must buy, build and manage it.

Replacing the PC

Microsoft has introduced tools and software that allow users to run applications that span private networks, Smart Devices and Cloud networks. An emerging capability will be the replacement of the Personal Computer, the PC, by Smart Device accessed Cloud computing facility. An example of this facility is "Google Docs". This Google provided "virtual" facility, via the Google Cloud, provides the equivalent facility of a PC executing Microsoft's Office Word Processing application program. There is essentially no limit on the ability of Cloud facilities to provide the equivalent of previous PC and packaged PC software functions, including Smart Device access.

Storage Options

Many vendors have announced Cloud storage Devices. However, the challenge is to find the right storage architecture to match your application needs. Most typically, the Cloud storage system uses 4 to 16 SATA (Serial Advanced Technology Attachment) Devices. They are linked together by software. It allows them to be accessed as a single entity, including Smart Device entry. The software handles drive failures. It keeps data on applications and end users. The capacities range from hundreds of terabytes to multiple petabytes.

The storage can be configured and add storage nodes. Capacity can be added as needed. Hence, capacity does not have to be purchased in advance. Cloud storage is best used for unstructured data such as images, drawings and documents. Software can direct storage in different geographical locations for backup. Date could also be structured by organizational responsibility and access limited to those approved for a given area. Accounting charges can be collected by functional area or responsibility.

Organizational Changes

Many existing data center and Smart Device skills will apply to Cloud systems. However, there will be a need for more collaboration cross disciplines. The systems administrator, the network manager, the mobile transaction management and the information security officer will need to collaborate up front. In the past their skills were applied at different times. With Cloud computing, coordinated actions require faster deployment and proper controls to avoid a spending spiral. In addition, Cloud computing will add a new set of issues, which the coordinated organization will quickly learn to handle, including Smart Device access.

Email

Shifting email services to a Cloud-based provider generally offers a quicker response to accommodating new users. The Cloud system assumes the burden of providing the latest software and effective software protection. Use of a Cloud facility allows the staff to spend more time rolling out new applications and helping new users. Use of the Cloud shifts the financial requirement from up front charges to paying as you go. All of these factors will contribute to the key Smart Device organization based objective of better financial control.

Taking advantage of the Cloud based email will require anticipating the type of email services required. These may range from mobile/ Smart Device based messaging to smaller or larger mailboxes. These needs must be provided in preparing the required email capacity and performance specifications. Software costs will include maintenance and support. Storage and archiving will accumulate over time and need to be anticipated. Staffing costs will require managing all elements of the system solution. The bank will find email/Smart Devices are a significant use of the Cloud facility.

Application Design

The three application components are: database; application processing; and user interface including Smart Devices. With Cloud computing these components are functionally independent. The application designer has the option of mixing on-premise and Cloud computing delivered system components. Optionally, all three components may reside on the same platform, at the designer's choice. Selected components may be moved later as the environment changes. Correspondingly, use of redundant resources will increase reliability. However, it also creates some security concerns.

Economics

With Cloud computing users avoid capital expenditures for hardware, software, and services. Users pay only for what they use. Consumption is billed on a utility basis (like electricity). Or, on a subscription basis (like a newspaper), with little or no upfront cost. Some Cloud providers now offer service on a flat monthly basis.

Other benefits of Cloud computing include a low cost barrier of entry, low management overhead and access to a broad array of applications. Users can terminate contracts at any time. However, services may be covered by agreements with financial penalties.

Cloud computing is similar to the displacement of electrical generator utilities in the early 20th century. Be careful, operating expenses may not save much over the savings on upfront capital expenditures. Likewise, the efficiency of a company's data center may be very competitive.

Security

Where is your data? How is it being protected? Who is accessing it? These are the Cloud security issues. Your data needs to be encrypted, backed up, often and where it is stored. It needs to comply with standards such as ISO 27001 (security controls to protect information resources). You need to ask for proof of staff approval, management processes and the technical infrastructure. These need to be demonstrated by independent audits and penetration tests, including Smart Devices. Your rights to these tests need to be included in your contract. (FOR DETAILED SECURITY MATERIAL SEE XLIBRIS BOOK "SECURE YOUR INTERNET USE").

Legal Pitfalls

Dozen of states and the federal court system require businesses to produce and retain digital records. That requires that Cloud computing vendors and solution providers write specific provisions for evidence discovery. There is also the legal issue of customers failing to pay for Cloud services. They face service cutoff of services, without access to any of their online resources. Can their data be held as collateral? Can their service agreements specify terms for various actions or omissions? The questions will be resolved with Cloud experience.

Concerns

Cloud computing introduces a new set of concerns. Can unauthorized users, including Smart Devices, get access to confidential data? What are the access rights of the data administrators? Can you establish access compliance policies, especially cross border? Do the disaster recovery procedures protect confidential data? Have you checked your techniques that establish separation of multiple customers' data in common storage areas? These and similar questions can be derived from your implementation plans.

Picking a Provider

The Cloud system provider is the key to good service. The provider should be reliable, well reputed and offer a proven record. There is a comprehensive database for "Cloud Computing Incidents Database (CCID)". This offers an opportunity to check a provider's adverse record, if any. The examination of the provider's record should also examine how he establishes backup and recovery processes, including Smart Device based applications.

Chapter iv-4

Smart Device Politics

Purpose: To alert the reader to the politics associated with Smart Devices

Action: Examine Smart Device offers carefully to understand the difference between genuine offers and tainted offers. (Tainted means using an old position while calling it a new one.)

Introduction: A Statement of Opinion by the Author

The fast and successful pace of Smart Device usage growth attracts a number of interested parties, especially those associated with previous technologies and market entries. All of the instruments associated with earlier solutions of the payment and marketing solutions will be impacted. Financial transaction cards, Smart (EMV) cards, ATMs, conventional retail marketing solutions, telephones, paper money, face to face financial branch transactions and the conventional cash register will all be impacted by the mobile Smart Device.

Aggressive, former industry groups will carve out a roll for them selves in this transition. For example, if their prior solution used integrated circuit chips, they will use that as evidence that they should automatically have a key role in the subsequent developments. That may not be entirely wrong. The Smart Device era will need standards. The Smart Device era will need a smooth transition from prior solutions. The Smart Device will be faced by many of the same problems of earlier solutions including fraud, illegal transactions, and costs. Hence, the experiences of prior implementations could be a valuable assist to the new Smart Device developments. That will not happen automatically !

The new mobile implementations offer new incentives.

The Value of Smart Device usage to the new user:

The mobile unit is personalizable for the user, providing the new user knows how to do that.

The mobile unit makes shopping more convenient, providing the new user knows how to achieve that.

The process is under the control of the user, only if the new user knows how to maintain Smart Device control.

The Value to the New Mobile Marketers, if they understand how to achieve the improved Smart Device marketing results:

Reduces transaction costs with Smart Device usage:

Reduces transaction costs and losses to fraud:

Improved customer targeting with marketing:

Gather better performance data with Smart Device use:

The Value to the Merchants with Smart Device usage:

Targeted offers to consumer required with Smart Device use:

Improved marketing approaches needed for Smart Devices:

Collect better usage data with Smart Devices:

The Issuers of Smart Device based offerings get:

Stronger brand images with Smart Device applications:

More relevant offers to Smart Device users

Derive better analytic data from their activities.

Carriers versus Associations Seek Smart Device Opportunity

VISA and MasterCard have independently acquired Organizations that specialize in "cards not present" transactions. These are essentially Smart Device based purchases. Three of the largest carriers in the United States, AT&T, T-Mobile and Verizon have announced a common effort to provide a mobile payment network, called "Soft". At the same time, Google has announced that they are developing a Smart Device designed to replace credit cards in mobile transactions. They stated an intent to develop the Smart Device to also replace cash, credit and debit cards, reward cards, coupons, tickets and transit passes. The network's services will be available to all merchants, banks and mobile carriers. The latter statement puts them into direct competition with the VISA and MasterCard networks.

The new Soft network has not announced prices, services, data bases, authorization process, and other network details. They will need to be evaluated versus the to be announced VISA and MasterCard mobile transaction plans and economics. To lead this effort the group chose the former chief marketing officer for credit cards at GE Capital.

All of the players in this move to Smart Device based network services have acquired resources with demonstrated know how in the application area:

MasterCard acquired DataCash for $ 520 M.

VISA acquired CyberSource for $ 2 B.

Soft was formed by three experienced carriers:

AT&T, T-Mobile, and Verizon.

Apple acquired Quatiro Wireless for $ 275 M.

Google acquired AdMob for $ 750 M.

Summary:

Recognize these actions are taking place in the formative stages of a new major industry move. Your understanding of the actions underway will allow you to better evaluate statements being made to sell products and services. Don't hesitate to ask penetrating questions as you interact with the new offerings. Your role will be to make the final decision—go or no go on propositions being offered for your implementation. Use these discussions to weigh the propositions.

Chapter iv-5

Payment Card Standards

Purpose: Describe the Payment Card Industry (PCI) standards effort

Action: Establish contact with the PCI SSC.

About the PCI Security Standards Council

The Payment Card Industry Security Standards Council was founded by five global payment organizations. They are American Express, Discover Financial Services, JCB (Japan Card International), MasterCard Worldwide, and VISA Inc.

The PCI DSS has six major objectives:

> Maintain secure networks in which transactions can be conducted.
>
> Cardholder information must be protected wherever it is stored.
>
> System should be protected against malicious hackers using frequently updated software.
>
> Access to system information and operations must be restricted and controlled.
>
> Networks must be constantly monitored and continually tested to ensure all security measures and processed are in place, are functioning properly, and are kept up to date.

A formal information security policy must be defined, maintained, and followed at all times and by all participants.

Enforcement of compliance and determination of any non-compliance penalties are carried out by the individual payment brands and not the council.

PCI Applications and Services

The PCI Web page (www.pcisecuritystandards.org) lists a variety of services and approved applications:

Validated payment applications (existing deployments):	89
Validated payment applications (new deployments):	772
Qualified security assessors	
Approved scanning vendors:	151
Internal security assessors	
PCI Forensic Investigators	

PCI Moves to a Three Year Review and Issue Cycle

Moving to a three year cycle for new standards review and issue gives merchants more time to understand them. It allows gathering more feedback. Also, to consider market reactions and emerging threats. If unexpected threats or other compelling reasons dictate a faster change, the PCI council reserves the right to move more quickly by issuing and "errata" notice.

Chapter iv-6

Smart Device "Keyless" Retail Transactions

Purpose: To describe work reducing Smart Device functions available.

Action: Use the work reducing steps in Internet based transactions.

Forty years experience with magnetic striped cards, used with self service units ranging from mass transit to Automatic Tellers, demonstrates why 80% of the world's population is implementing self-service transactions in all industries. By contrast, 72% of our population are shopping on the Internet, but only 15% shop with multiple vendors. The need is for a "Keyless Internet Transaction" structure which can be understood and repeated with ONE use. That was the prime success factor for magnetic striped card use.

Transactions on the Internet remain complex. A retail purchase requires up to 25 steps. Half of the steps require data entry keying and three steps require users to examine the results of long search responses. The use of improved solutions such as Amazon's "1 click" reduce these efforts by one half, which is still 12 steps and 2 searches.

Conventional Internet Transaction

Placing a conventional retail transaction through the Internet is a 15 to 20 keyed steps process. The process would include these steps:

1. Search for a search engine.
2. Select a search engine.
3. Search for a vendor.
4. Select a vendor.

5. Search for a desired item to be purchased.
6. Select the item to be purchased.
7. Select the item's style.
8. Select the item's size.
9. Select the item's color.
10. Select the quantity.
11. Select the delivery method.
12. Select delivery option.
13. Enter delivery address and postal zone.
14. Confirm acceptance of the total charge.
15. Select payment alternative.
16. Select credit card to be used.
17. Enter payment amount information.
18. Approve payment process and amount.
19. Print invoice and shipment information.

The Smart Device Introduces New Function

The Smart Device based, keyless process starts with information stored in the Smart Device. Included are: (1) The user's preferred payment information; (2) The user's preferred shipping requirements; and (3) the user's preferred email address for communications.

"Frequent Favorite" is a new form of browser based function which provides direct Internet access, generally listed in a sequence of URL's. When one is selected, it provides an appropriate Internet web page address (URL). The URL automatically directs the user's Internet browser unit to the web page describing the article, service or subject being considered for acquisition. Use of this feature bypasses the need for using search engines and scanning long streams of search results. Without any keying, the browsers presents the web page showing the URL identified item. Beyond that, the order options, e.g. color, size and so forth, are selected by using a mouse. The order completion information for payment and shipping are provided by Smart Device stored content.

Keyless Shopping Speeds Purchasing Internet Acquisitions

This Smart Device supported function is a time savor. By bypassing the need for searches and examining search outputs is a browser function provided by most browsers. Your use of this Smart Device supported function will substantially speed your Internet access and getting results on a more timely basis.

Chapter iv-7

Traveling with Smart Devices

Purpose: describe international requirements for using a Smart Device

Action: Prepare for an international trip with solutions for the Smart Device international requirements.

Smart Device Traveling Support

Historically, traveling meant leaving your entertainment Devices at home—your music, your books, your reference materials, your movies and your TV. Today, they all travel with you, thanks to the Smart Device and networks. In addition, your Smart Device provides important assistance on your travels. Included with your Smart Device travel support are:

1) Handling emergencies: The Smart Device allows browsing the Internet for emergency support contact numbers. These important emergency support contact numbers are accessible to any manufacturers' Smart Device with an Internet browsing function. In most countries, the emergency services also provide for English language speaking access in addition to the local spoken language. The emergency services also use international graphic signs which are readable on your Smart Device display.

2) Finding a public restroom: All Smart Devices can access a universal application "sitorsquat.com". Enter your geographic location or postal zone. The Smart Device application will display the name and location of the public restrooms in your area. Also included is the street map to facilitate finding your

travel route to the facility of your choice. The days and hours of access are not shown.

3) Locating a Restaurant or Retail Establishment: Most Smart Devices have available an application program which locates local restaurants on a local street map, after entering the physical location or postal zone number. Some applications include reviews of their offerings to assist the Smart Device user to make a selection. The locations include name, address and are superimposed on the local street map to facilitate local travel.

4) Staying productive while traveling: There are a variety of Smart Device applications available for writers, accountants, business owners and other Smart Device users which allow them to keep working while traveling. They can continue to develop their materials. Then, they may be forwarded by the networks to their point of usage. At the same time, the networks may be used remotely for search and research necessary to complete their work effort, even if away from their usual work location. However, watch your phone charges.

5) Hotels are creating better room keys by using Smart Device's wallets to hold room keys. You can open room doors by holding your Smart Device next to a door lock. This allows you to bypass the front desk and going directly to your room. This avoids us of magnetic stripes which become demagnetized. Use of the Smart Device as a room key also allows the hotel to check your arrival.

World Phones

The GSM (Global System for Mobile Communication) is a type of Smart Device used in Europe and most world countries. T-Mobile and AT&T use the GSM in the United States, but many USA carriers do not. GSM based phones can be used throughout the world.

Smart Devices may be "locked" to a given carrier. Their internal program allows usage of the Smart Device only with a designated carrier. They may be "Unlocked". There are firms which have the equipment to unlock the Smart Device.

Unlocking should be performed before traveling. It allows you to change SIM cards and use the Smart Device in different countries.

Each Smart Device has a SIM (Subscriber Information Module) card. It contains the identification of the Smart Device and the account identification for carrier designation. The SIM cards can be easily changed physically. Hence, when traveling, you need to acquire SIM cards for the countries in which you plan to use your Smart Device. They are not expensive and give you access to the local telephone charge rate. However, buying a SIM card in Italy requires a 72 hour registration process.

Why do you need a Smart Device while traveling? Many vacation rentals do not provide a telephone or phone service. The Smart Device is very helpful when traveling with others when they are staying at a separate facility. It allows easy coordination of movement arrangements.

Your travel options for travel outside your country of origin include these alternatives:

1. Purchase an unlocked GSM phone and SIM in the country where you plan to stay.

2. Rent a phone locally with the correct SIM.

3. Use your GSM phone locally by having it Unlocked and purchasing the correct SIM locally.

The European Smart Device situation changes constantly. Rather than attempt to keep up, buy or rent the current solution upon your arrival. Buying a local solution also provides you with free reception of calls.

Note: In the UK it is difficult to find unlocked GSM Smart Devices. It is better to bring one with you.

Before renting a phone in Europe check what country the Smart Device is registered in. Get one for the country of your planned visit. If it is a different country you may incur long distant charges for each "local" call. Always ask for the local per minute charge for the Smart Device you rent, if you pay for incoming calls, what country the Smart Device is registered for, and if Voicemail is available to take messages.

Internet based companies offer rental Smart Devices for European usage:

> cellularabroad.com: provides GSM phones and SIM cards. Use promo code "SLOWTRAV" for a US$ 10 reduction.

> telestial.com: provides GSM phones and phone cards. Use promo code "SLOWTRAV" for a 10% discount on all purchases.

> contextrome.com rents GSM phones and SIM cards for Italy.

There is an expensive advantage using your USA Smart Device in Europe. You can be reached easily by dialing a USA phone number. You must get the calling charges and whether you pay for incoming calls for the country of use. You must check the power setting required for charging your Smart Device. If the transformer is marked 100-240V then it will work in Europe without damaging the transformer. If not, get a transformer locally. Most hotels have them.

Dialing international telephone numbers must be preceded by an international calling code to assure reaching the right country and phone number. In the United States the code for international calls is 011. However, preceding the number being called by a + will automatically dial the international code.

There are a number of fine tuning points in dealing with international calls. A good internet reference is "slowtrav.com/Europe/cell_phones". Review the content for some finer details.

Dealing With Airport Headaches

Traveling can be difficult. There are a number of Smart Device applications that can be helpful. Download these to help with your trip:

google.com/mobile/maps: This application offers road directions and road conditions. Red indicates heavy congestion. Black indicates stop and go conditions.

m.smartparkJFK.com: Allows searching for available reserve parking spots at JFK airport in New York. This save a lot of time. Several Smart Device applications will take you to your car. Two $0.99 applications are findmycar and takemetomycar. anresgroup.com

flighttrackpro takes your flight number or route to learn your flight's status, gate and aircraft type. tripit is a popular trip management service. It alerts you to flight delays or cancellations. It also provides a list of flight options with status and available seats. mobiata.com updates you on flight changes.

flightcaster.com: helps with a flight cancellation. Plug in your origin, destination and travel date. It will produce a list of alternative flights for more than 1200 carriers. Get detail airport layout and shop location information from ifly.com/iphone-pro or touchmeme.com/nextflight.html.

Negotiating the security arrangements is aided by tsa.gov/travelers/mobile. It will help you locate the checkpoints. Also, provide answers to most commonly asked security questions.

If you need to book an airport hotel or a rental car on the fly try orbitz.com/mobile. kayak.com/mobile provides much of the same information access on the move.

duckduckmoosedesign.com will keep your child occupied with colorful illustrations and songs on your Smart Device. Another is virtual-gs.appspot.com.

Smart Device Based Boarding Passes: United Airlines issues a Smart Device based boarding pass. The Boarding pass QR code is displayed on the Smart Device display. That display is read by the airline's departure gate optical readers. Any last minute changes can be reflected in a changed code. They are being read at 20 airports and their points of acceptance are increasing.

Smart Device Applications Make Automobiles Safer

Smart Device applications are being used to make automobile driving a much safer endeavor. They are offered with the admonition that you are to keep your hands on the steering wheel and your eyes on the road, for safety sakes:

trapster.com: locates police speed traps. It is welcomed by the police as an aid to slow traffic.

skobbler.com: provides the same type of voice directed navigation for cards without navigation systems.

point.com: searches for auto service stations by price or location.

cheapageas.com: list auto stations by gas price, within 10 miles. You have to search by location.

apps.usa.gov/alternative-fuel-locator: shows all types of fuel stations and their business hours.

weatherbug.com: gives local weather and road conditions for where you are going.

nadaguides.com and edmunds.com: let you build car models, and compare prices.

chrysler.com plans to have free app manuals for all their cars.

Happy Smart Device travels !

about the author

Jerome Svigals is a long-range banking and transaction card strategies consultant to major international banks and card servicing companies. He leads top bank management teams in preparing five-year goals and plans for their financial services and card-related products. Clients have included Commonwealth Bank of Australia, Hongkong and Shanghai Banking Corporation, Canadian Bank of Commerce (CIBC), Lloyds Bank (London), Citibank Development, the Prepaid Card Corporation of Japan, the three major banks of Brazil, three smart card vendors, the Finland PTT, Intel Corporation, and Price Waterhouse. He was ranked by the "American Banker" newspaper as one of the top 25 United States banking industry consultants.

Mr Svigals has been an advisor to government and industry groups on electronic banking and card-technology trends including the US Congress, the US Treasury, the Department of Justice (on crime in EFT systems), the Department of Agriculture (on food stamp automation), MasterCard (on smart card tests), and the Credit Card Bankers of Thailand (on new card media alternatives and economics). He was the first president of the PC Memory Card International Association. He advised on the formation of the Smart Card Forum.

Invited speeches have included ESCAT (International director), SCAT Conferences (Program director), EFTPOS, Payphone Association, Australia Plastic Card (Chair), Pan Asia Smart Card Conference (Chair), BAI Retail Delivery Conference, ID Expo, Brazil Bankers Convention, Bellcorp Transaction Conference, Australia Smart Card Conference (Chair), Lafferty Retail banking Conferences (London, Miami, Milan, Singapore and Sydney), ATM Banking in South-East Asia, and Future Branch Planning in South-East Asia. He has spoken at more than 300 finance industry conferences.

He served as a vice-president and strategic planning officer for the Bank of America. Mr Svigals served as a Senior Planning Officer for the Lloyd's Bank, City of London, England. He has authored books on planning for electronic banking for Macmillan, on Smart (EMV) cards from McGraw Hill, and Bank Branching 2010, Smart (EMV) cards 2010, and Retail Bank 2025 for Lafferty Publications. His articles have appeared in Price Waterhouse's "Five Year Projections" and Auerbach Publishing "Data Security Series".

Employed by IBM until he retired, Svigals served in several executive positions. He was the assistant director of marketing for the domestic data processing company. He was the marketing executive on the 13 person team that created the IBM 360 system. He was systems manager for the Asia/Australia portion of IBM World Trade Corporation. He introduced the IBM 360 system to the 15 IBM country organizations comprising the IBM World Trade Asia/Australiarea.

Mr Svigals was a senior manager in IBM product development. He led the IBM team that developed the first international standard magnetic striped cards and tickets. He ran the world's first test of the standard striped magnetic media (plastic cards and airline tickets) using the first interactive self service equipment for American Express, American Airlines and IBM. Mr Svigals' card development library has been acquired by the Computer History Museum, Mountain View, California. See Youtube

(Svigals Computer History). He was chosen as the Alumnus of the Year 2009 by the Engineering School Alumni of the City College of New York, for career achievements.

Mr Svigals was the IBM Senior Banking Industry consultant, world-wide. He consulted for the senior management of most of the world's largest banks, on five continents. Mr Svigals was a chair of the US national subcommittee on electronic retail banking standards (ANSC X9A), and first chair of the US working group (ANSC X3B10.1) for Integrated (Smart) Card technology standards. He was a member of several ISO standards working groups. He is a board member of the Silicon Valley Round Table of the National Association for Business Economics.

www.ingramcontent.com/pod-product-compliance
Lightning Source LLC
Chambersburg PA
CBHW051232050326
40689CB00007B/891